Bookends

Activities, centers, contracts, and ideas galore to enhance children's literature

by

Michele Borba
and
Dan Ungaro

illustrated by Michele Borba

Cover by Vanessa Booth

Copyright © Good Apple, Inc. 1982

ISBN No. 0-86653-065-7

Printing No. 987654321

GOOD APPLE, INC.
BOX 299
CARTHAGE, IL 62321-0299

With love to Jason,

May your future
be bright, beautiful and
filled with books.

Table of Contents

Dear Teacher,

This book is a collection of ideas, activities, centers and independent learning contracts. The book can and should be used to fit YOUR needs and the needs of YOUR STUDENTS. You may choose to use each suggestion
    ...with a large group OR a small group,
    ...for the entire class OR for individuals,
    ...as an assignment OR as a free-choice activity.

Most teachers will agree that one of the most delightful times of the day is the story hour. It's such a cozy time for teacher-class togetherness. Watching children's faces as they react to the story characters' dilemmas is a hard experience to beat. This book has been written to help you increase these experiences. Literature is so enriching, it certainly does not have to be limited to the story hour. Ideas in this book will help you make literature part of the total classroom curriculum. Contracts, centers and activities have been designed for using literature for
    ...an individualized reading program,
    ...reading aloud to the children,
    ...exploring books in depth,
    ...social studies - exploring foreign countries,
    ...science concepts,
    ...bibliotherapy self-esteem,
    ...enrichment tasks as follow-ups to reading,
    ...just pure enjoyment.

Book suggestions to use with special topics appear throughout the pages. You may use the books mentioned or feel free to adapt other books of your choice.

We hope that this book will help to provide a contagious reading spirit with your students so that a frequent request, "May I read it again?" can be heard from them.

Michele Borba   *Dan Ungaro*

NOTES

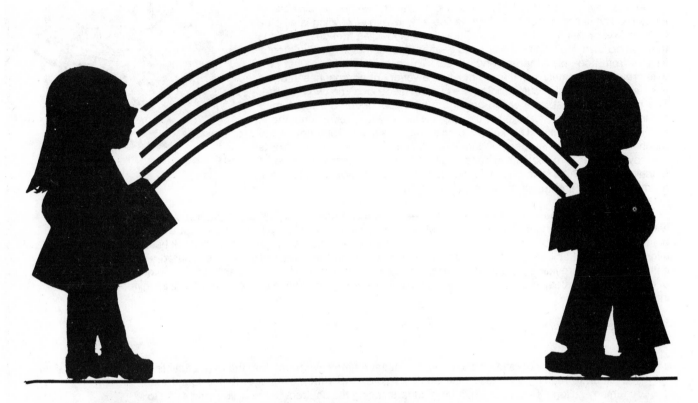

1 : Books, Rainbows and Me

Activities, work sheets, and tons of ideas to make the world of books enjoyable for children:

For the Love of Books
Book Nooks
Selling Books
The Story Hour
Books They Like
Book Ideas

And Still More!
And Word Ideas...
And More!
One More Time
Book Checklist
Let's Find Out

For the Love of Books

An old saying, "if a little bit is good, a lot is better," is most applicable as far as reading is concerned. The bottom line for the love of reading is when a child makes books a part of his life. They are included as friends. He reads them on his own. He gains a therapeutic treatment for some physical or mental ailment from book bibliotherapy encounters. The bits and parts of what provides reading love means that there must be a variety of approaches in order to assure that this will occur. Children are custom-made jobs - no two are alike. The reading act must be a varied one if the individual needs are to be met. Meaning, experience, imagery, sounds, visual attack, and kinesthetic methods all play a role. The key to putting this mishmash together is the teacher. The parents, lay people, and librarians can help, but the teacher is the key. The modern teacher of reading must use a hydromatic method of teaching as she shifts from one technique to another to provide a smooth ride to understanding and to assure a love for reading.

The goal of this book is primarily to help teachers make use of the variety of approaches needed without fragmentizing them. This multiplicity of procedures must bring into play all of the resources possible to simplify the task of the teacher. The child must be relaxed and eager, for as biofeedback has found, mind efficiency takes a giant step forward when there is lack of tension and success is assured. Parents can play a role in providing a great deal of help. Authors, illustrators and librarians can help to promote love of reading. Finally, sleep learning can increase the joy of learning and hence a love for reading if imagineering is utilized.

Teachers can promote a love of books in a variety of ways:

1. Provide a story of reading and of books. Researchers have found that the main stumbling block to reading success is the **abstract** quality of written language. It was found that many children had great difficulty in understanding the abstract terms which adults use to talk about language, for example "word," "letters," "sound," etc. Many children are like quicksilver - the more you try to grasp or trap them, the farther they spurt. The story of reading will clear things up for children. An illustrated story of reading is provided in *Imagineering the Reading Process.*

2. Make books a part of your room. Book centers can provide the motivation to look and to want to read various displayed books.

3. Expose children to the beauty of books. Children are attracted to books in many ways other than by the words. Maurice Sendak, the noted children's author and illustrator, tells of his first book. It was given to him by his sister at age nine. He says there is so much more to a book than just the reading of it. He first set the book up and just stared at it for a long time; it was a beautiful object. Then came the smelling of it. He also stated that he bit it to gain a taste. The last thing he did was read it. Robert McKim, of Stanford, believes one reason Johnny can't read is that he isn't seeing very well. McKim feels that children are not exposed to the pictures of books. They are to illustrate concepts, but too often, due to lack of time, etc., class exercises are keyed to rapid naming, to the detriment of observing. A suggested list of beautiful books for parents to buy to start an early exposure to beauty is included in another section. You may want to use these to further expose your children.

4. Have books make up a daily part of the room activity. Begin the day with a story. The Reading Aloud section covers this procedure and has a suggested list of books.

5. Share new children's books that are meaningful to you. Share your favorite childhood books.

6. Allow book-sharing parties. Children can also share their favorite books as part of the show-and-tell time.

7. Give books to children at Christmas time, for birthdays, as get well gifts or as a going away memento for a moving child.

8. Provide a "free reading time" in your class. Each child keeps an ongoing book he is reading in his desk for after recess, before lunch, and during lull times.

9. Provide a Guided Enrichment (Individualized) Program. This is covered in another section.

10. Provide book suggestions for parents.

11. Have a field trip to a special book store. Each child can bring money from home to buy a favorite book.

12. Have a Book Week in your room during the time that this occurs nationally. Have the librarian review the new Caldecott and Newbery books.

13. Invite an author or an illustrator of children's books to the class. These human resource people can provide a tremendous step for creating a love of books.

14. Have interested children write to an author. The publishers of a favorite book will be happy to forward the letters. Maurice Sendak tells of the pleasure he received when a first grader wrote to ask if he could visit *Where the Wild Things Are!*

The activities in this section are designed primarily to help teachers and to help embroider in the library of the children's minds a lasting love for books.

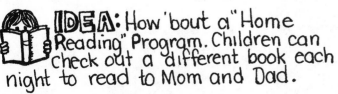
IDEA: How 'bout a "Home Reading" Program. Children can check out a different book each night to read to Mom and Dad.

Book Nooks

A comfortable room environment should be essential for the "reading" classroom. Ample room space should be available for displaying and storing books. They should also be accessible for browsing and reading. A comfortable environment will definitely be more conducive to the reading spirit.

Begin by setting up your classroom with frequent classroom reading in mind. You may wish to set up a cozy reading corner for children to slip away to and read, read, read. Carpets, pillows, rocking chairs and couches may be some kinds of furniture you'll wish to include. Don't rule out the possibility of a reading loft! Parents can be very helpful in supplying (and building) many of the items you'll need if you will let them in on your desires. A bunk bed can also become a fun reading space if you can find one to have donated.

To store your books, bookshelves will definitely be high on your list of needs. Consider a few options such as these for displaying classroom books:

- the tops of shelves
- hanging books over a clothesline strung tightly along a wall
- storing a few class favorites in picnic-size baskets at the reading center
- propping crates on top of each other to store books inside
- setting boards on top of large bricks to use as a bookshelf
- setting a few books in the chalk trays beneath the chalkboard
- along window sills
- tabletops, tabletops and tabletops
- paint holders beneath the paint easel
- magazine racks
- ask stationery stores to give you their discarded card holders
- propped up to bulletin boards
- propped up on nails or hooks along walls, doors or screens

Selling Books

There are various techniques to "sell" a book to children. Here are a few to keep in mind:

A book corner containing a variety of books attractively arranged can well become an oasis to start the process of quenching the thirst of interest.

Try to display your books face out. Book jackets are designed to grab the child's attention and to invite skimming. If the jacket is hidden or removed the value of the sales appeal is lost. Colorful and ridiculous pictures appeal to children. The Dr. Seuss books have tremendous appeal because of the amusing pictures. Seeing an elephant perched high on a tree sitting on a nest is ridiculous. The picture immediately grabs the eye and the attention of the child. Needless to say, he is sold!

Some books, of course, can be displayed flat on a table. Children can then be free to browse through them and "feel" their contents.

Keep some of those special books for special occasions in reserve for such classroom events as lost teeth, new shoes, the death of a class pet, a new student, or special holidays and seasons.

Set aside a special time each day or week for sharing a new class book. You can make the book appealing by telling a little about the plot or characters and showing a few colorful pictures. Be sure to then show the students where the book can be found for them to look at and enjoy on their own.

Above all, nothing will sell children onto books more than seeing, feeling and hearing them over and over. Make books a part of your daily classroom plan. Consider beginning and/or ending the day with a story. Whenever a special occasion comes up, celebrate with a good book. Each child can also keep his favorite book or a book he is currently reading in his desk. Anytime there is an opportunity to read, children can then pull out their books and continue to enjoy their stories.

IDEA: How 'bout a Read-a-Thon? Each child can bring a bag of books and a pillow to sit on. Now spend the whole day reading!

THE STORY HOUR

One of the best ways to interest children in books is to read to them. Teachers can do a great deal to "sell" books. In many ways you can become a sort of a "con artist," similar to those we used to see at the circus. Once a child has heard a good book read aloud, he can hardly wait to savor it again! There are many ways to "sell" a book. Here are a few:

CREATE AN ATMOSPHERE
Children should be seated comfortably and close to the teacher so that all may see the pictures easily. This will enable them to identify with the characters and action of the story. Illustrations should be shared and savored since they are such eye and interest grabbers.

VOICE COMMUNICATION
Try to find time to rehearse the story before reading it to the children. Your voice is an instrument for communicating the author's meanings. Your tone and pitch are important elements in helping to instill the children's interest.

INTERACTION
Try to hold off any discussions until the story is completed. Following the story, an avid discussion can take place. Questions should be of the type which will create involvement. Try to make these be open-ended and thought provoking such as those illustrated in the "Guided Enrichment" section.

DON'T SHUT THE DOOR
We're all aware that children can get caught up by the infectious nature of the words, rhymes and tempo of the story. Encourage children to interact with author's words as the story is read. Little children love to say "If you don't watch out!" to "Little Orphant Annie" by James Whitcomb Riley or "I'll huff and I'll puff 'til I blow your house down!" to "The Three Little Pigs." Children will also respond to humor and rhyme as well. A reading of "Horton Hatches the Egg" by Dr. Seuss will have the children repeating, "Faithful, faithful, one hundred per cent" each time it is read.

BOOK SELECTIONS
Books should be carefully selected with your students' interests and age levels in mind. Try not to select books that the children are reading avidly. The story hour is the time to stretch imaginations, extend interests and to develop an appreciation of fine writing. A wonderful technique to create interest in a book is to invite an upper grade class to dramatize a story for a primary class. This is great fun for both groups, particularly if it is broadcast over the intercom. Don't forget to invite your principal and other staff members in to periodically read to the children, too. A list of books children love to listen to is included. The list, though, is endless! Just elicit the suggestions of your students!

BOOKS THEY LIKE

First Grade

Bailey, Carolyn, *The Little Rabbit Who Wanted Red Wings*, Platt & Munk.
Gag, Wanda, *Millions of Cats*, Coward & McCann.
McCloskey, Robert, *Make Way for Ducklings*, Viking.
Potter, Beatrix, *The Tale of Peter Rabbit*, Warne.
Slobodkin, Louis, *Caps for Sale*, W.R. Scott.

First and Second Grades

Bemelmans, Ludwig, *Madeline*, Viking
Bishop, Claire, *The Five Chinese Brothers*, Coward & McCann.
Duvoisin, Roger, *Petunia*, Knopf.
Duvoisin, Roger, *Veronica*, Knopf.
Flack, Marjorie, *The Story About Ping*, Macmillan.
Fatio, Louise, *The Happy Lion*, Whittlesey.
Freeman, Lon, *Dandelion*, Viking.
Lindgren, Astrid, *The Tomten*, Coward & McCann.
Sendak, Maurice, *Where the Wild Things Are*, Harper & Row.
Silverstein, Shel, *The Giving Tree*, Harper & Row.
Steig, William, *Sylvester and the Magic Pebble*, Simon.
Tworkoy, Jack, *The Camel Who Took a Walk*, Dutton.
Zion, Gene, *Harry the Dirty Dog*, Harper & Row.

Third Grade

Edmonds, Walter D., *The Matchlock Gun,* Dodd, Mead.
Kipling, Rudyard, *Just So Stories*, Doubleday.
Lionni, Leo, *Tico and the Golden Wings*, Pantheon.
Lionni, Leo, *Swimmy*, Pantheon.
Seuss, Dr., *The 500 Hats of Bartholomew Cubbins*, Vanguard.
Wilder, Laura Ingalls, *Little House on the Prairie*, Harper & Row.

Fourth, Fifth and Sixth Grades

Barrie, J.M., *Peter Pan*, Walt Disney Classics, Grosset & Dunlop.
Blume, Judy, *Freckle Juice*, Yearling.
Dahl, Roald, *Charlie and the Chocolate Factory*, Knopf.
Defoe, Daniel, *Robinson Crusoe*, Charles Scibner's Sons.
DuBois, William, *The Twenty One Balloons*, Viking.
Grahame, Kenneth, *The Wind in the Willows*, Scribner.
Lewis, C.S., *The Lion, the Witch, and the Wardrobe*, Macmillan.
MacDonald, Betty, *Mrs. Piggle Wiggle*, Lippencott.
MacDonald, Betty, *Mrs. Piggle Wiggle's Farm*, Lippencott.
Milne, A.A., *Winnie the Pooh*, Dutton.
Norton, Mary, *The Borrowers*, Harcourt.
Rockwell, Thomas, *How to Eat Fried Worms*, Watts.
Seredy, Kate, *The Good Master*, Viking.
O'Dell, Scott, *Island of the Blue Dolphins*, Houghton Mifflin.

IDEA: Arrange a time each week for the principal to read to the class.

BOOK IDEAS

There are so many things you can do to help promote an enjoyable book climate, as well as make books meaningful to children. Here are a few ideas to try:

FOR ESPECIALLY FUN BOOK PROJECTS YOU COULD
...start a CLASS BOOK TOWER by stacking boxes or ice-cream cartons on top of one another. Each time someone finishes a book he may add his name and the book title to the tower.
...decorate the classroom by making LARGE STUFFED PILLOWS of storybook characters.
...have a READING PARTY and invite guests in to see all the special book projects as well as listen to everyone read a special favorite part from his favorite story.
...have a CLASS CAMPAIGN FOR THE "BEST BOOK." Each group can design their own campaign posters, bumper stickers and campaign buttons, as well as have campaign speeches on why everyone should vote for their choice of the favorite book.
...have a BOOK EXCHANGE. Everyone can bring in a book from home he no longer wants and exchange it with a friend.
...join a class BOOK CLUB.
...visit a BOOKSTORE. Everyone can bring money from home to buy a new book together.
...have everyone write his own books. See "How to Make a Book" in this chapter. Invite the school librarian and principal to the room. They will view the books and decide which books are the CALDECOTT (best illustrated) and the NEWBERY (best written) AWARD WINNERS in the class. Special ribbons can be given.
...WRITE A LETTER to your favorite classroom artist or illustrator.
...visit a PRINTING SHOP or a PUBLISHING HOUSE to see how books are made.
...start a READING GARDEN in your room. Each time someone finishes a book he may make a colorful paper flower and pin it to a bulletin board or above the chalkboard. On the flower write the book title and the child's name.
...keep a CLASS BOOK SCRAPBOOK. Each time a story is read to the class, a child may critique it in the scrapbook.
...give BOOKS AS GIFTS for Christmas, birthdays, get well wishes, moving away, the end of the year and special times.
...INVITE YOUNGER CHILDREN to the room to share a special book project.
...SET ASIDE A TIME EACH DAY WHEN EVERYONE READS A FAVORITE BOOK.

TRY ALSO
...choosing any three words in the story. Can you make them into a phrase...sentence...paragraph...story?
...choose any 10 words. Can you make up a crossword puzzle using them all?
...making up your own definitions for the words. Now look them up. How close were you?
...writing a word...now think of a synonym for it...how about an antonym...homonym.

AND MORE IDEAS!

AFTER READING ABOUT ANOTHER COUNTRY

...design a travel brochure for the country.
...draw the flag and seal of the country.
...make a time line showing special events.
...bring in a recipe for an authentic dish.
...visit a travel agency and collect travel posters.
...also collect information and pamphlets.
...make a map of the country.
...write an announcement about an historical event.
...collect pictures and charts.
...write a time capsule summary. Pretend you lived during the time written in the book. What was it like?
...make a milk carton vehicle showing the kind of transportation that was used in the story.
...find a song or some music about the country. Share it.
...bring in an object mentioned in the story.
...write an epitaph for a famous countryman.
...write an invitation to visit the country.
...write to the embassy for information.
...draw a picture of the national flower.
...learn to count from one to ten in the native language.
...make a bulletin board display for the room.
...what authors or illustrators were born in the country? Bring in their works.
...find out about the government today.
...what stories are written about the country? For instance, "Stone Soup" is about Russia and "Umbrella" is about Japan.
...what famous artists are from the country? Bring in copies of their art.

INSTEAD OF DRAWING YOUR FAVORITE PART OF THE STORY YOU COULD MAKE A

...mural
...banner
...collage
...stitchery
...mobile
...scroll theater
...movie
...book jacket
...wall hanging
...mosaic
...book quilt
...comic strip on adding machine paper
...peek box
...book cube
...scene in a ham can, a pie tin, a paper plate, a shoe box or a meat tray.

INSTEAD OF A BOOK REPORT MAKE

...a commercial about your book
...a want ad
...a billboard
...a book mobile
...an award (why it's so super)
...a book jacket
...a book review
...a bumper sticker
...a campaign button
...a bulletin board
...a news bulletin
...a wanted poster
...a cartoon
...a telegram
...a jingle
...a skit
...a comic strip
...a book rhyme
...a letter to a friend
...a pamphlet
...a puppet show
...a poster
...a tape recording
...a song
...new titles
...a puzzle
...a description
...an oral reading
...a pantomime
...an advertisement
...a game of charades

AND WORD IDEAS...

YOU COULD ALSO LIST WORDS THAT

...are short
...are long
...are nouns
...are verbs
...are adverbs
...begin with a special letter (b, d, f...)
...end with a special letter (k, ck, q...)
...begin with a blend
...begin with a vowel
...begin with a consonant
...have a special vowel pattern like aw, au, oo
...have 1 syllable or 2, 3, 4 syllables
...have lots of tall letters
...have lots of short letters
...are found in the beginning, middle or end of the dictionary
...you know how to read
...are capitalized
...are compound words
...are contractions
...you like or don't like
...have endings
...have prefixes
...make sounds
...you can touch, feel, taste, smell or see
...are serious
...are happy
...are sad
...show color
...are found in the city or the country
...are animals
...are people
...are names
...are seasonal
...are musical
...are silly
...make you feel good
...are proper nouns
...you'd like to use again

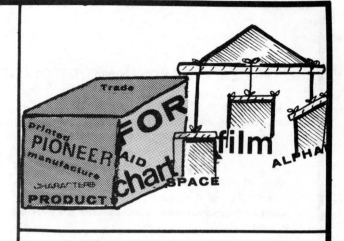

YOU COULD ALSO TRY USING YOUR WORDS IN A

...headline
...banner
...announcement
...commercial
...menu
...want ad
...silly singing
...letter jingle
...poem
...slogan
...song
...riddle
...bumper sticker
...campaign button
...fortune
...direction
...quotation
...tongue twister
...obituary
...valentine
...fairy tale
...myth
...tall tale
...mystery

INSTEAD OF WRITING EACH WORD FIVE TIMES YOU COULD

...make a "WORD CUBE"...cover a box with words you like
...make a "WORD MOBILE"...hang words from a stick, dowel, or hanger
...keep a record of your words on a WORD GRAFFITI paper
...COLLECT NEW WORDS in a scrapbook, recipe file box, diary, your own dictionary, a notebook, index cards or on adding machine tape.

BOOK CHECKLIST

Books open the doors to many new worlds. They can be about many interesting and colorful things. Can you find one of each of these books? Write the titles on the lines below.

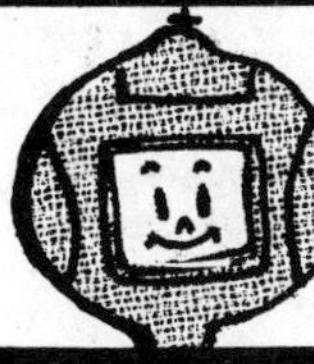	science fiction ____________________	
	fairy tale ____________________	
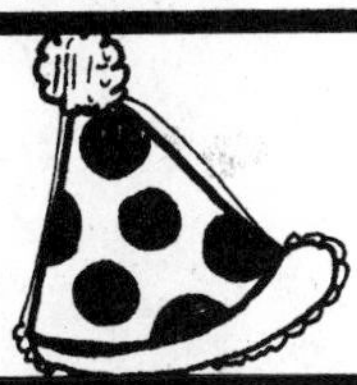	comedy (funny) ____________________	
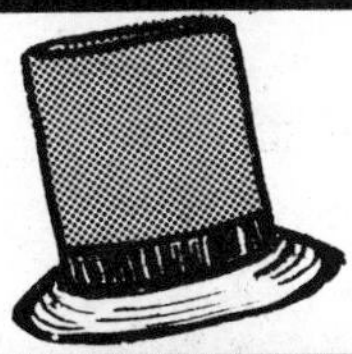	biography ____________________	
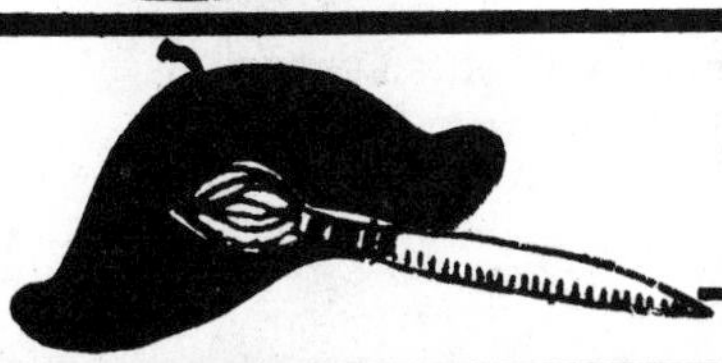	picture book ____________________	
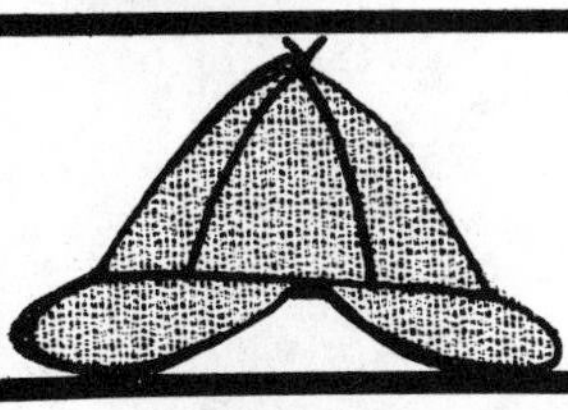	mystery ____________________	
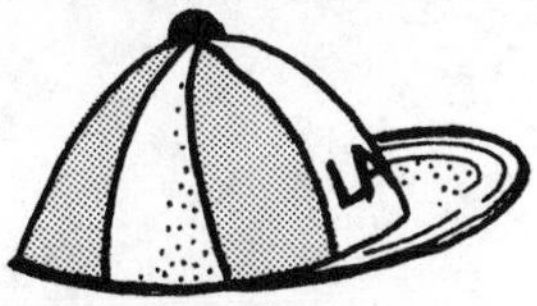	sports ____________________	
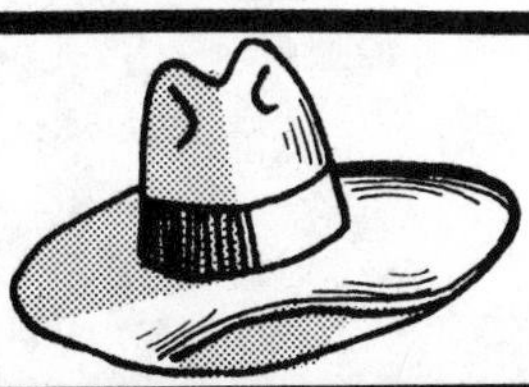	adventure ____________________	

AUTHORS ARE PEOPLE, TOO!

Books can become more meaningful to children as you explain the parts of books and how they are made. As children begin to understand more about the book's writer the author can become much more real to the children. There are many ways you can do this. Here are a few ideas:

Tell children a little about the author's life. Information can be gathered from the book jacket or from library reference books.

Most authors love to receive mail. Why not write favorite classroom authors letters as part of a weekly or monthly class project? Children can ask them questions or tell them why they enjoy their books. Authors can be written in care of the publisher. A list of publishers and their addresses has been included in the "Guided Enrichment" chapter.

Display additional works of the author you are currently reading about. Children can then compare their books. A few authors (and there are hundreds!) who have written many children's favorites include:

Maurice Sendak	William Steig
Beatrix Potter	Don Freeman
Ezra Jack Keats	Bernard Waber
Marie Hall Ets	Robert Kraus
Leo and Diane Dillon	Nonny Hogrogian
Peter Spier	H.A. Rey
J.R.R. Tolkien	Pat Hutchins
Leo Lionni	Margaret Wise Brown
Russel Hoban	Miriam Cohen
Robert McCloskey	Mercer Mayer

and the list goes on and on...

Enlist the help of community human resources. Invite a local author to visit your class. Children will enjoy learning about firsthand experiences of an author, as well as finding out about the process of bookmaking.

Have a "Favorite Author Day"! Each child can choose his favorite author and share a few of his works with the class. At the end of the day be sure to vote on the favorite author of the class.

Set aside a permanent area in your room for displaying the works of favorite authors. Pictures of the authors can be cut from the book jackets and a bit about their lives can be included below each illustration. As letters come to the class from authors, they can be proudly pinned to the display.

The Author

The author is the person who wrote your book.

1. What is the name of your author?

_____

2. Is the author a man or a woman?

_____

3. what is the title of the book your author wrote?

_____

4. List other books your author has written.

_____
_____
_____
_____

5. Find out about your author.

_____
_____
_____
_____
_____
_____
_____
_____
_____
_____
_____

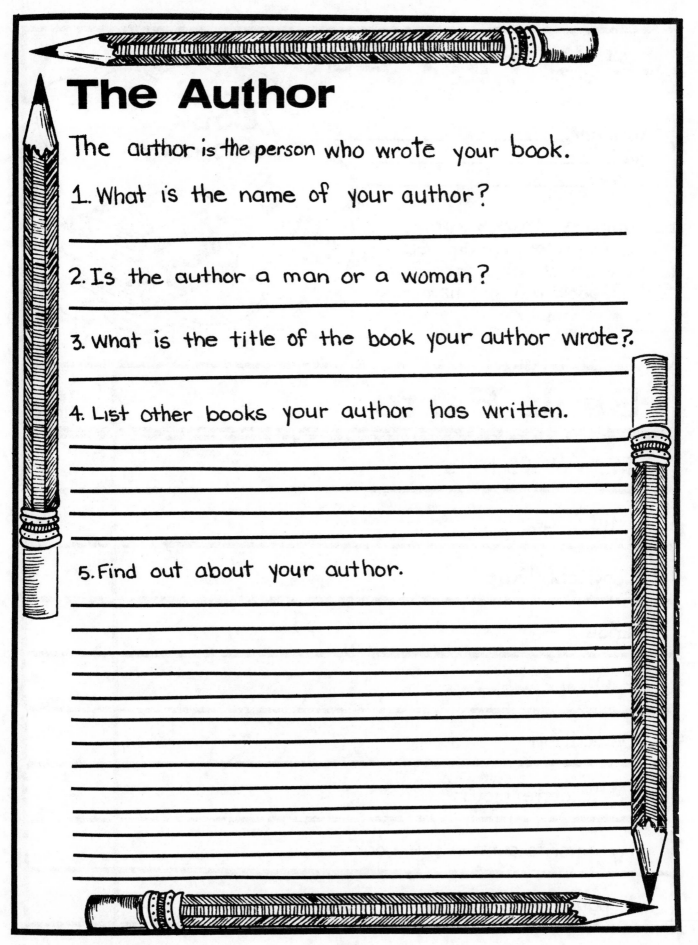

Let's Find Out

Book
Discovery

Examiner: ____________________
Title: ____________________
Author: ____________________

Examine your book carefully. On what page did you find each of these parts? (Your book may not have all of them.)

Book Parts	Page Number
Table of Contents	
Title Page	
Copyright Date	
Index	
Publisher	
Dedication	
My favorite picture	
My favorite part in the book	
A page which has a new word	

2: ENRICHING BOOKS

Activities, book lists, record sheets, and organizing steps for individualizing reading.

Organizing a Guided Enrichment Program

Steps to a Guided Enrichment Program

The Reading Steps

The Reading Record

The Reading Express

The Book Report

Guided Enrichment Reading

To organize your Guided Enrichment Reading Program, follow these steps:

Step 1   Begin saving books, books, books!

Parent donations can be a valuable source.

The school library and city libraries are other excellent sources. Try to collect books of varying topics and levels.

Step 2   Sort the books into different reading levels.

The levels should be appropriate for the reading abilities in your room. Paint or cover boxes with different colored paper to represent different reading levels. Each level can be color coded for easy reference with a piece of colored masking tape on the side of the box.

Step 3   Prepare sets of questions.

For each book used in the G.E.R. Program, you may wish to type out questions on index cards. These cards may be stored in a library pocket glued to the cover page of the book. For books you check out from the library, store the cards in a permanent file box in alphabetical order for quick reference. On each card, list stimulating questions with page references and sets of words, also with page references. You can then guide the reading with ease. Word checks for sight vocabulary and phonetic analysis could be quickly made, also. Since the questions and words have page references, you will be able to check the child's comprehension, thinking, etc., during the various phases of the reading.

A sample list of cards that are ready to be used for the program have been included in the back of this section. Two cards have been included for each book. The top section contains a synopsis of the book with words and page references. The bottom card contains a list of comprehension questions to ask the child. The cards are ready to be cut out. The two sections should be folded together. They may be added to your file box or stored in the pockets pasted in the books.

Step 4   Set a special time for reading books only!

During this time children may browse through the class library to choose books and settle down for a period of silent reading. A list of the reading steps for each child to follow is included on the next page.

Step 5   Fill in the Reading Observation Record.

Sometime during the reading period, the teacher or child may record the title of book read, the dates of starting and the completion. A reproducible example of the Reading Record can be found in this chapter.

Step 6   Schedule an individual conference.

At the completion of the book, the child and the teacher meet for a conference. This is the time the teacher can check the child's comprehension, vocabulary, oral reading, phonetic performance and other skills. Use the Observation Record form to keep the notes on individual meetings. A reproducible example of the Observation Record form can be found in this chapter.

Step 7   Record and report on the book.

After the individual conference where the child has demonstrated comprehension of the book, the child must complete a book report or activity (see the following pages about book reports in the Book Report chapter, or use the Book Report form in this section). The child may then record the book title on The Reading Express work sheet.

Step 8   Reward their progress.

Helping children see their progress is an important key to ongoing motivation. As a child completes a book report or masters a new reading skill or concept, recognize him with a special badge award, or give him a chance to share his book in a special way.

17

THE READING STEPS

1 Choose your book.

2 Read it to yourself.

3 When you're stuck with a word...

a Try to sound it out.

b Read the whole sentence with the word in it.

c Does the picture give a clue?

d Quietly ask a friend.

e Quietly ask the teacher.

4 Read the book to the teacher. Answer the questions.

5 Write your book report.

6 Turn it in to the teacher.

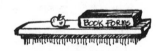

7 Put your book away.

The Story About Ping
By Marjorie Flack and Kurt Wiese

High second - Low Third
Viking Press

A story of the adventures of Ping, a beautiful duck. Ping did not want to be the last to go aboard the boat they lived on because the master gave the last one on a spanking. Ping is late one day, but does not go aboard. He almost ends up as part of a dinner, but a little boy turns him loose because he is too beautiful to eat. Ping has learned his lesson and takes a spanking.

Words:

Yangtze (2)	swooped (13)
marched (3)	barrel (16)
scurrying (4)	beautiful (23)
crossed (7)	

Questions:

1. Why did the ducks leave the boat each day? (They had to hunt for things to eat.)
2. Can you guess why Ping did not hear the call to go home? (Because he was wrong side up trying to catch a small fish.)
3. Do you think Ping learned a lesson? (Yes, he was willing to get a spanking when he was last in line.)
4. Can you guess why some of the ducks are yellow and some white? (The young ones are yellow.)

Millions of Cats
By Wanda Gag

High Second - Low Third
Faber & Faber

A story about a lonely old man and a lonely old woman. She thought that a cat would solve the problem. The little old man said he would get her a cat, and he did - hundreds of cats, thousands of cats and millions and billions and trillions of cats.

Words: (Pages not numbered in the book)

flowers	million
quarrel	trillion
scratched	billion
clawed	frightened
	valley

Questions:

1. Why couldn't the little old lady and the little old man be happy? (Because they were lonely.)
2. How did the little old man and the little old woman decide which cat they would keep? (They decided to let the cats decide which one was the prettiest.)
3. What words do you think would best describe the cats? (They were selfish and jealous.)
4. Do you think that the little old man was as smart as the little old woman? (No, he didn't realize that they couldn't feed so many cats.)
5. How did it happen that the little kitten was not eaten by the other cats? (He thought he was homely, so when the cats were asked who was the prettiest he didn't say anything so nobody bothered about him.)

19

Stone Soup
By Marcia Brown

High Second - Low Third
Charles Scribner's Sons

This is a story about three tired, hungry soldiers who outsmarted the peasants. They were given things needed for a soup after they had suggested making soup from stones. They were also given beds in the best homes because they were clever.

Words: (Pages not numbered in the book)

trudged	hungry
impossible	buckets
peasants	fetch
villagers	
	entertained
	require
	splendid
	barley

Questions:

1. Why didn't the people want to feed and board the soldiers? (They were afraid of them and thought they would take all of their food.)
2. What reasons did the peasants give for not feeding the soldiers? (They said they had used the grain for feed, they had sick to care for, all too many mouths needed to be filled.)
3. Do you think the soldiers were smart? (Yes, they suggested making a stone soup. It aroused the peasants' curiosity.)
4. Were the soldiers greedy? (No, they shared the soup and were willing to sleep in the loft.)

Don't Count Your Chicks
By Ingri & Edgar Parin D'aulaire

High Second - Low Third
Doubleday

A story about the old American proverb, "Don't count your chickens before they are hatched." A woman has one hen who lays an egg every day. She lets her imagination take over. Soon she has a suitor, servants, milk and many other things that will result from more hens after she sells the eggs from the one hen. She realizes that being proud does not bring happiness. She is happy to return home to the one hen and an egg a day.

Words: (Pages not numbered in the book)

crowed	counted
replied	thought
wonder	finished
figure	neither
	lonesome
	beamed
	mistress
	suitor

Questions:

1. Why was the rooster crowing when the sun wasn't up? (He said he had opened his eyes and soon the sun would be up.)
2. Why was the woman so pleased with her hen? (It laid an egg every day and other hens lay once in awhile.)
3. Why did she start to think? (To make the time go faster.)
4. Do you think what she was thinking was possible? (No, she only had one hen and it would take a long, long, long time for so many more eggs to be hatched in order to buy what she planned.)
5. Do you think she was too disappointed? (No, she wondered why she had become so proud, and she was happy to be home with what she had.)

Sammy the Seal
By Syd Hoff

First Grade
Harper and Brothers

This is a delightful story of a seal who wants to see what it is like outside the zoo. He promised to return soon. He made some mistakes. He tried to swim in a bathtub. When he saw some children in line at a school he joined them. After a day in school he was eager to return.

Words:

animals (7)	where (20)	once (35)
food (7)	have (21)	voices (42)
empty (14)	everything (25)	sounds (43)
that (14)	stranger (26)	all right (49)
there (14)	lovely (28)	caught (56)
wrong (16)	water (29)	belong (60)
know (17)	place (33)	welcome (63)

Questions:

1. Can you think of some words to describe Sammy? (He was sad (16). He was curious (17). He was a good, polite seal (18). He was smart- he found a place to swim (33)). He was sorry (35). He was wise - he learned he belonged in the zoo (60).

Mike Mulligan and His Steam Shovel
By Virginia Lee Burton

High Second - Low Third
Houghton Mifflin

This is a story about Mike Mulligan and his beautiful steam shovel. Her name is Mary Anne. Mike said she could dig as much in a day as a hundred men could in a week. Mary Anne and other steam shovels were being replaced by the new type of shovels. Mike did not want Mary Anne to be sold as junk. She had a last chance to prove that she could dig as much as a hundred men in a week.

Words: (Pages not numbered in the book)

canals	straightened	everywhere
through	skyscrapers	settled
lowered	deciding	happened

Questions:

1. Why do you think Mike said that Mary Anne could dig as much in a day as a hundred men if he wasn't quite sure? (Because he was very proud of her.)
2. Why do you think Mary Anne did not grow old after many years and after much work? (Mike took such good care of her.)
3. Do you think that Mr. Swap was a fair man? (No, he wanted to make certain that Mike Mulligan did not get paid.)
4. What helped Mary Anne and Mike to dig faster? (The large number of people who came to watch and encourage them.)

21

The Five Chinese Brothers
By Claire Bishop and Kurt Wiese

High Second - Low Third
Coward - McCann

An old Chinese folk tale about five brothers who looked exactly alike, but one could swallow the sea, one had an iron neck, one could stretch his legs, one could not be burned and the fifth could hold his breath indefinitely. When the first got into trouble and was sentenced to death by various means, he cleverly exchanged places with his brothers and so it was impossible to get rid of him.

Words: (Pages not numbered in the book)

swallow	indefinitely	finally	obey
treasures	iron	caught	condition
sign	uncovered	extraordinary	algae
disappeared	execution	fantastic	attention
condemned	assembled	innocent	comfortable

Questions:

1. Is this a true story? (No, such things are not possible.)
2. Was the little boy obedient? (No, he would not come back.)
3. Would you say the first Chinese brother used good judgment? (No, he should not have let the little boy wander away when he swallowed the ocean.)
4. Why do you think the little boy refused to come back? (He was so attracted by the many new things to see when the ocean was swallowed that he probably could not hear the call or see him beckoning. The Chinese brother soon had a mouth full of ocean, so he could not call him.)
5. Would you say the first Chinese brother was innocent? (No, he was responsible for the little boy becoming lost.)

Danny and the Dinosaur
By Syd Hoff

High First - Low Second
Harper & Row

A make-believe story about a little boy, Danny, and his visit to a zoo. He imagines that the dinosaur could play with him. They visit many places and have some exciting things happen in the city.

Words:

museum	voice (11)
Eskimos (6)	policeman (15)
swords (7)	delighted (41)
dinosaur (9)	wonderful (64)

Questions:

1. What did Danny love? (He loved dinosaurs.)
2. What did he wish he had? (He wished he had a dinosaur.)
3. How did Danny help people in the neighborhood? (He helped people at the bus stop, helped them to cross the street, and he had the dinosaur carry the bundles.)
4. How did the children make the dinosaur feel good when they were playing hide-and-go seek? (They made believe that they could not find him.)
5. Do you think that Danny was wise? (Yes, he realized that they would not have room for a pet that size.)

Alexander and the Wind-Up Mouse
By Leo Lionni

High Second - Low Third
Knopf/Pantheon

This is a fascinating story of two mice, Willy and Alexander. Willy is a mechanical mouse who is loved by everyone. Alexander is a real mouse who envies Willy because everyone is always chasing Alexander away. A magic lizard promises to change Alexander into a mechanical mouse if he can find a purple pebble. Alexander finds the pebble but has Willy changed into a real mouse.

Words: (Pages not numbered in the book)

scream	adventures	quivering
directions	hideout	almost
ordinary	cuddled	rustled
favorite		mysteriously

Questions:

1. Do you think Alexander envied Willy? (Yes, because everyone chased him and Willy was loved.)
2. Is this a true story? (No, a mechanical mouse could not talk.)
3. Do you think Alexander was wise in doing what he did? (Yes, because if he had become a mechanical mouse he would have been thrown away.)
4. Do you think Willy was happy that he was no longer a mechanical mouse? (Yes, he would not be thrown away, and he and Alexander danced until dawn to show they were happy.)

Ox-Cart Man
By Donald Hall

High Second - Low Third
Viking Press

This is a Caldecott award-winning book about a New Englander and his family. The story tells of life in the early colonial days. The family loads their ox-cart with everything they made or grew all year long that was left over. The man then takes the cart to the Portsmouth Market to sell all of the goods. He also sells the cart and his beloved ox. He then buys various goods and provisions to start the process over again.

Words: (Pages not numbered in the book)

everything	carved	barrel
sheared	borrowed	embroidery
linen	honeycombs	Barlow
shingles	turnips	wintergreen
		peppermint
		whittling

Questions:

1. When do you think this story took place? (During the colonial days.)
2. Why do you think the ox-cart man had to take his things on such a long trip? (In those days they did not have stores except in the large cities.)
3. Can you think of two things which showed he loved his ox? (He did not ride on the cart as he did not want to overwork the ox. He kissed him good-bye after he sold him.)
4. If he loved the ox, why did he sell him? (They needed the money for supplies and he had another young ox at home.)
5. What proves he was a kind, considerate man? (He walked to the market. He bought extra things for the family. They missed him and they all were happy to help, so it shows they liked him.)
6. What was different about the lives of children in those days and with your life? (They all had to help to provide food. They had to make and sew the things they needed.)

23

The Snowy Day
Ezra Jack Keats

High First - Low Second
Viking Press

The quiet fun of a small boy's adventures in the deep snow brings out a child's delight. Peter makes tracks in the snow, knocks off snow from the branches, makes a snowman, and finally fills his pocket to take some home. Imagine his surprise when he finds the pocket empty!

Words:

during (7)	thought (19)
covered (7)	enough (19)
high (9)	angels (21)
pointing (10)	pretended (22)
slowly (12)	

Questions:

1. Why was the snow piled up along the street? (To make a path for walking.)
2. What did Peter make in the snow? (He made tracks.)
3. If you were looking for Peter, do you think you could find him? (Yes, because you could follow his tracks.)
4. Why didn't he join the big boys? (He wasn't old enough.)
5. Do you think he lost the snowball he put in his pocket? (No, it melted.)
6. How do you know he was not sad that his dream was not true? (He was smiling when he saw the snow was still everywhere.)

The Biggest Bear
By Lynd Ward

High Second - Low Third
Houghton Mifflin

A Caldecott story about a little boy who goes looking for the biggest bear in the woods. He finds a cub who soon grows into a BIG bear who gets into a great deal of trouble. He loves the sugar, syrup, apples and other foods at the farm. Johnny's father says the bear must go. The bear loves Johnny and they have a very hard time trying to get rid of it. Finally, the bear ends up in a zoo.

Words:

farthest (3)	shelves (34)	prisoners (72)
direction (6)	wonderful (38)	whenever (78)
humiliated (12)	emptied (40)	tribulation (46)
surprised (22)		

Questions:

1. Why do you think grandfather ran away from the bear in the orchard? (He didn't have a gun since he was picking apples.)
2. Why do you think Johnny was humiliated? (The other barns had a bearskin hanging.)
3. Was Johnny the kind of a friend you would like? (Yes, he was brave and kind to the bear. He was also understanding when his father explained the bear had to go.)
4. Why do you think the bear would not stay in the woods? (Johnny and his family had been kind to him.)
5. Why do you think Johnny took a gun when he took the bear into the forest? (It was a part of the forest he had never seen before.)

24

Harold and the Purple Crayon

High First - Low Second
Scholastic

Harold and the Purple Crayon
By Crockett Johnson

A story about Harold, a little boy who takes a fantasy trip with his trusty purple crayon. He makes roads, paths, boats, ships and a balloon to help him. He encounters a terrible dragon, but he is able to escape with the aid of his purple crayon and ends up in his bed.

Words: (Pages not numbered in the book)

farther
mountain
crayon
straight

moonlight
suddenly
remember

Questions:

1. What did Harold decide to do one evening? (He decided to go go for a walk.)
2. Name five places Harold went. (A field, a forest, an ocean, a beach, a hill and a mountain.)
3. What did Harold suddenly remember? (He remembered where his bedroom window was.)
4. What do you think Harold was probably doing? (He was probably dreaming.)

Inch by Inch

High First - Low Second
Scott Foresman

Inch by Inch
By Leo Lionni

A story of how an inchworm outsmarts the nightingale. He fools the nightingale by telling him he will measure his songs. While the bird sings, the worm crawls away.

Words: (Pages not numbered in the book)

emerald
heron
flaming

pleasant
toucan
measure

Questions:

1. What part of the heron did the worm measure? (The legs.)
2. What did the nightingale want the worm to measure? (His song.)
3. Did the inchworm think he could measure the song? (No, he knew this was impossible.)
4. Can you think of why the inchworm was able to outsmart the bird? (He knew that the song of a nightingale is long and he could inch away. He also knew that while the bird was singing he would not notice the inch-worm as he inched away.)

Observation Sheet

Date	Word Knowledge	Phonetic Analysis	Oral Reading	Critical Thinking
Student				

Reading Record

Name

Title	Date Started	Date Comp.

BOOK REPORT

Title _____

Author _____

Choose a way to show your favorite part of the story.	
Paint	Draw
Clay	Cut and Paste

Write 1 or 2 sentences about why you enjoyed the story.

Choose a few words from the story that you thought were interesting and helped paint a "word picture" for you.

a "peachy" day

The Reading Express

leader

title:

29

BOOK AWARD

Presented To:

_____

Date:

_____

Official Signature:

_____

3: BOOK BINDERY

Centers, task cards, activity cards and charts to enrich classroom literature.

The Book Report Center
Book Report Chart
Book Mobiles
Covers
Book Critic
Letters
Book Ads
Character Study
Bookmarks
Bag Puppets
Super Sleuth
Titles
Book Sharing
Commercials

Dioramas
Story Parts
Character Hangings
Riddles
Masks
Movies
The Tale End
Real or Make-Believe?
Book Plates
Bookends
Book Covers
Book Banners
Make a Book
Book Bindings

BOOK REPORTS

Colored Paper

Lined Paper

Tracing Paper

Plain Paper

BOOK REPORTS

GLUE

DINOSAURS

HEIDI

FLOWERS

Shoe Boxes

IDEA: Have a Reading Party! Each child can invite *his* favorite "significant other" to come. Have special book projects on display for parents to view. Children can then curl up in a corner with Mom or Dad and read together.

BOOK IDEAS

There are many fun learning projects children can do as follow-up activities to their reading. Ready-to-use book activities are included in this section for your classroom use.

Book Center

Set up a permanent area in your room as a Book Center. Materials for book projects as well as new books to display may be set up.

Book Report Chart

A large chart with ideas for book reports is included in this section. Display the chart at the center as an idea source for children to use in planning their book report follow-ups.

Activity Cards

Twenty-four activity cards are included in this section for use at the Book Center. Cards may be mounted on durable paper such as tagboard for use as task cards. The cards may also be duplicated for individual use by providing a copy duplicated for each child.

Large Activity Cards

Several full-size activity cards are also included. These can be duplicated for each child or hung at the Book Center for children to do.

BOOK REPORT

Retell the story by making a Scroll for the Scroll theatre.

Create a Flannel-board story from a favorite part.

Make a paper bag puppet to show one of the main characters.

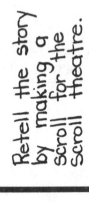

Make a dio-rama of your favorite book scene.

Write a story and make puppets to tell about your book.

Give a commercial in class on why you should read the book.

Make a book cover for your book.

Think of riddles for 5 words you found in the book.

You and a friend put on a skit about a favorite part.

Read your book to a friend.

Paint a picture of your favorite part.

Read your favorite page to the class.

BOOK MOBILES

1

1. Cut out at least 4 shapes. The shapes can be about something in the book.

2. On a different shape tell the name of your book, tell about a character, tell what happened in the book, tell why you liked the book.

3. Tie your shapes to your hanger.

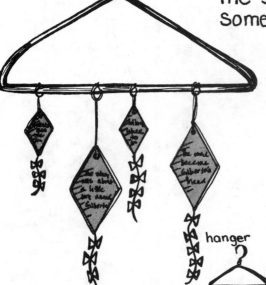

hanger   crayons   scissors   string

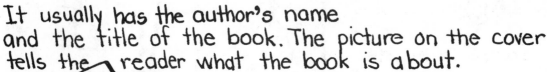

PAPER

COVERS

2

1. Look at the cover of your book.

It usually has the author's name and the title of the book. The picture on the cover tells the reader what the book is about.

2. Design a new cover for your book. Include the title and the author.

Paper

Book Critic

(3)

Review the book you just read.

1. What did you like about the book?
2. Did the pictures give you a hint about what was to happen in the story?
3. What did you learn in the book?
4. What changes would you have made in the story?

Letters

(4)

1. Write a letter to tell a friend about the book you have just read. Tell your friend why he or she might like to read it.

2. Use the letter form to help.

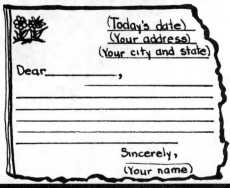

(Today's date)
(Your address)
(Your city and state)

Dear _____ ,
_____
_____
_____
_____

Sincerely,
(Your name)

BOOK ADS

⑤

1. Pretend you are writing a want ad for the newspaper. How will you sell people your book to read?

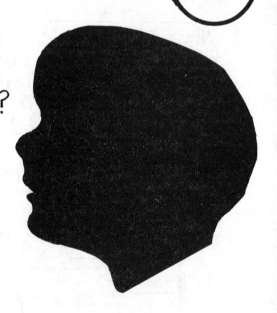

2.
Write your ad on paper.

Character Study

⑥

1. Investigate one of the characters in your book.

2. Answer these questions...

What was the character's name?
Did you like the character?
Why or why not?
Where did the character live?
What did the character do in the story?

3. Write your answers.

Bookmarks

1. Make a bookmark for a book you have read.

2. Write the title and author of the book on the bookmark.

You need:

BAG PUPPETS

1. Make a bag puppet of one of the characters in your book.

2. Draw part of the character's mouth on the top flap of the bag and part of the mouth on the side under the bottom flap.

3. Add features to the face. You could use
   * paper   * noodles
   * yarn   * egg carton pieces
   * pipe cleaners * material
   * wallpaper   * feathers

Super Sleuth

Can you solve these questions?

1. Who were the main characters?
2. Where did the story take place?
3. When did the story take place (now, a long time ago, in the future)?
4. What was the story about?

TITLES

1. A title is the name of the book. It tells the reader something about the book. Peter Pan is the title of a famous story.

2. How many other titles for your book can you think of? Write them.

BOOK SHARING (11)

1. Do you have a special book you've read that you'd like to share?

2. Sign up as a storyteller!

   Let the teacher know which day you'd like to share your book.

COMMERCIALS (12)

Write a commercial about the book you read. Try to "sell" the book so that another friend would like to read it.

Sign up for a performance date.

DIORAMAS

13

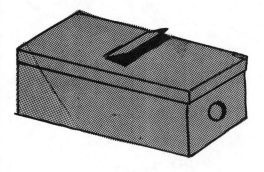

1. You need a box with a removable lid.
2. Cut a small peephole in the side of the box.
3. Cut along 3 sides on the top of the box. Fold the slot back for light.
4. Make a scene from the book inside the box.

Story Parts

14

A story is like an animal.
It has 3 parts.

a beginning   a middle   an end
Can you remember the three parts of the book you just read? List them.

Character Hangings

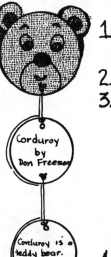

1. Make a paper head of a main character.

2. Cut a few big circles out of paper.
3. On each circle write something about the character.
   - What was the title of the story he/she was in?
   - What did he/she look like?
   - What did he/she do in the story?
   - Would you like to know him/her? Why?
   - Was he/she a real or make-believe character?
4. Punch a hole in the middle of the top and bottom of the circles and head.
5. Tie 5"-yarn pieces in the holes to connect the ⊙s.

You need— paper punch

15

RIDDLES

16

WHAT AM I?

I am soft.
I have button eyes.
I am brown.
You buy me in a store.

1. Choose a naming word (noun) from your story.
2. Write a riddle about it on your paper.
3. Cut a folding door on your paper. Only cut three sides of the door. The door can open and close.
4. Draw a picture of your name word on another piece of paper. The paper should be a little bigger than the door.
5. Paste the picture on the back of your door. Close the door!

You need : scissors  crayons   9"x12" 2"x3" paper pencil

MASKS

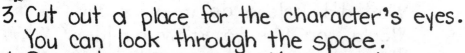

17

1. Make a mask of one of the characters in your book.
2. Cut out a circle a little bit larger than your face. Use heavy paper.
3. Cut out a place for the character's eyes. You can look through the space.
4. Decorate your mask. You could use

* paint	* buttons	* tissue paper
* crayons	* noodles	* cotton
* felt-tipped pens	* crepe paper	* construction paper
* yarn	* yarn	* lace
* ribbons	* wallpaper	* anything else!

MOVIES

Stone Soup by Ann McGovern

1. Make a movie of your book!
2. Cut a long strip of butcher paper 3" x 36".
3. Roll each of the ends around a pencil.
4. Tape the ends to the pencils.
5. Use crayon, colored pencils or watercolor pens to draw scenes from the story.
6. Roll your movie up to tell the story to a friend.

The Tale End

1. The ending is the last part of the book.
   How did the book end?
   Was it...
   ...happy...sad...mysterious...silly...make-believe?

2. How else could your book have ended?
   Write a new ending to your story.
   Do you like your ending better than the
   author's ending?

REAL OR MAKE-BELIEVE?

1. Was your story real
   or make-believe?

2. How do you know?
   List at least 3 reasons
   you think the story was
   real or make-believe.

BOOKPLATES

(21)

Make your own bookplates to glue inside your books. You could use such things as:
  * gummed labels
  * construction paper

1. Carve your initials on
   a linoleum block
   an eraser
   a styrofoam block.
2. Ink your initials with
   a stamp pad
   thick tempera paint
   printing ink.
3. Print your initials by pressing the design onto your paper.
4. Decorate your plates with felt pens, cutouts, or stickers.

BOOKENDS

(22)

1. Make sets of bookends for your favorite books. You could make them from:
   old bricks, oatmeal cartons, chicken barrels, shoe boxes, milk cartons, or cereal boxes.
2. Fill the containers with sand so they will be heavy enough to stand up.
3. Decorate your bookends with odds and ends like:
   enamel paint or marking pens
   buttons and yarn
   felt cutouts
   Con-Tact paper or wallpaper
   glitter and sequins
   beads and feathers
   pipe cleaners
   cardboard

BOOK COVERS

(23)

1. Make a cover to protect a favorite book. Have fun designing your cover. Here are a few ideas for you to use: gift-wrapping paper, comic pages, material, maps, construction paper, felt, wallpaper, con-act paper.
2. You may wish to decorate your cover with
   glitter
   sequins
   felt pieces
   crayons
   construction paper
   yarn
   ribbons
   stitchery
   stickers

←2"→ ←—————→ ←—→ ←2"→
         ½"

book length plus ½"

BOOK BANNERS

(24)

1. Make your own banner for the book you read. You could make it from cardboard, construction paper, material, or wallpaper.
2. Decorate your banner with pictures about your story. You could use paint, paper cutouts, stitchery, yarn strips, felt-tipped pen, or crayon.
3. Hang your banner in a place where everyone can see it! Hang it with clothespins, clothes hangers, a dowel or yarn.

MAKE A BOOK

1

Put the pages neatly in a pile.

2

Staple the pages in three places ¼ inch from the edge.

3

Make a cover for the book. You could use wallpaper, gift-wrap, material, Con-Tact or colored paper.

4

Fold the cover over the pages. Staple the cover again along the same edge in three places.

5

Cut a colorful strip of plastic tape or paper the length of the pages. Fold the strip lengthwise and fold it over the staples.

6

Decorate the cover carefully. Be sure to write the title and your name on the outside for everyone to see.

BOOKBINDING

1

Put the pages neatly in a pile.

2

Fold the pages in half.

3

Hammer five thin nails through the fold of the paper.

4

With a needle and thread, stitch back and forth through the holes. Take out the nails as you sew.

5

Tie off the string and cut off any left over.

6

Cover two pieces of cardboard with fabric, wallpaper or gift wrap. Glue them on.

Leave about 3/4" space between the covers. Join the front and back covers together with adhesive cloth tape.

BOOK COVERS

1

You need:
  scissors, felt, your book.
Measure the book on the fabric. Cut the fabric the length of the open book plus eight inches.

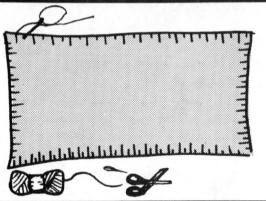

2

You need:
  scissors, a large needle, wool yarn, fabric.
Edge the piece of fabric with blanket stitches.

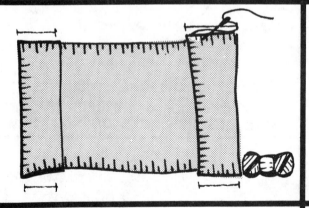

3

You need:
  scissors, large needle, wool yarn, fabric.
Fold both ends of your fabric over about 4". Measure the fabric folded in ½ to see if it's about the same size. Whipstitch.

4

You need:
  glitter, sequins, yarn, glue fabric, stitchery, material.
Decorate the front cover of the fabric. Fold the fabric in half and slip in your book. Keep the cover for yourself or give it as a gift.

4: SPOTLIGHT ON BOOKS

Activities and ideas to make books come to life!

A Puppet Center

Puppets - Puppets - Puppets

A Puppet Theatre

Puppet Stages

Make a Puppet

Puppet Play

Books for Plays

Masks and Things

..Puppets...Puppets...Puppets.

Puppets and children just naturally seem to go together. That special kind of gleam always seems to emerge in children's eyes as soon as they place puppets on their fingers. Why not capitalize on this built-in enthusiasm and incorporate puppetry as part of your "literama" curriculum? By having supplies available at a puppet center, children can turn book plots into delightful class puppetry productions for all to enjoy.

A puppet center as shown on the following page can easily become part of your classroom with just a few furniture changes. Designate an area in your room for the center to be permanently established. You probably will want to have a large table surface available as a work space. Provide a few easy books on puppet making for idea starters. A chart of puppet suggestions is also included in this section for sparking additional puppetry ideas. The chart may be placed at eye level at the center as a reference guide.

Supplies for making puppets may be stored in boxes, laundry tubs, ice-cream cartons or baskets. Parents can be a great source of help in providing or refreshing puppet supplies. Some items you may wish to include for puppet trimmings are those listed in the "Parent Help" letter.

IDEA: How about a character party? Each child can come dressed as a favorite storybook character.

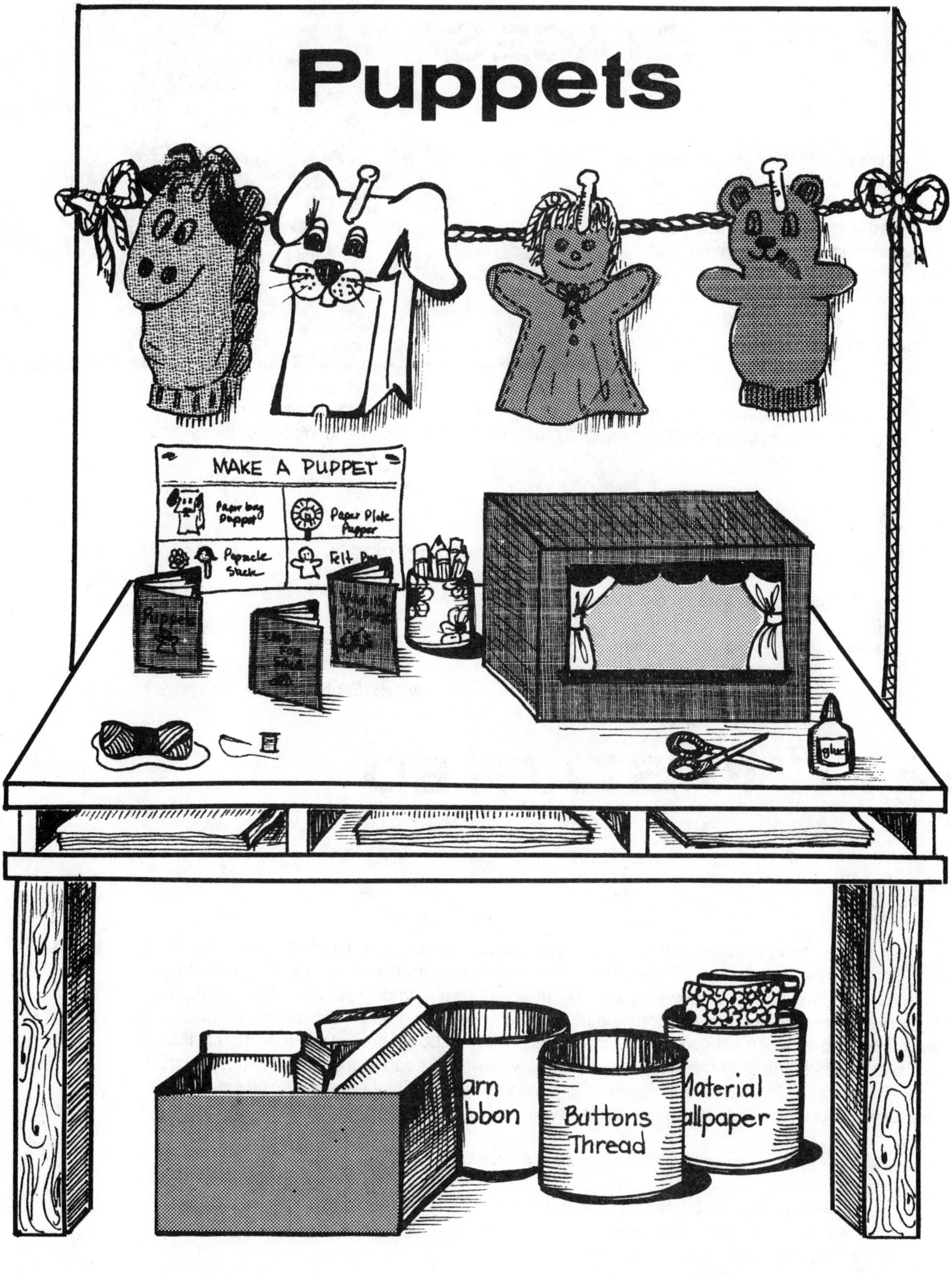
Puppets
MAKE A PUPPET
Paper bag Puppet
Paper Plate Puppet
Popsicle Stick
Puppets
glue
Buttons
Thread
Material

PUPPET STAGES

A puppet theatre is an item you'll probably want to include as part of your classroom repertoire. Many educational companies have beautiful ready-made theatres that are available for purchase. If your funds are short, there are many alternatives that can still serve your purpose nicely. Some of these include:

An old sheet hung from a wire in your classroom. Cut an opening in the sheet for children to perform through. Children can also paint it colorfully for shows. Fold it up after each performance and store it for the next time.

Turn a table sideways. Children can kneel behind it.

Move a classroom bookcase temporarily to the center of the room.

Remove the insides from an old TV set.

Cut an opening in a box that is large enough for children to get inside of.

Cut an opening in the bottom of a shoe box and turn it sideways. Each child can then have his own puppet theatre for finger puppets.

GETTING STARTED

Almost any child's favorite can be readily adapted to puppet plays. Old folk tales and children's classics such as "Henny Penny" and "The Three Billy Goats Gruff" are always enjoyable standbys. Once a child has chosen a book to dramatize, the next step is to decide which type of puppet will best represent the story characters. Sometimes the easiest puppets, such as the Popsicle-stick kind, are the best since an impromptu performance may then be presented while interest in the story is still at its peak. The child can then work individually or with a group in preparing the puppet production. Filling out the "Puppet Time" form in this section may be helpful since it will remind the child of the tasks he or she needs to complete before giving the final show.

A few book favorites you may wish to choose from could include:

Andy and the Lion by Daughtery, Viking Press.
Ask Mr. Bear by Flack, Macmillan.
One Fine Day by Hogrogian, Macmillan.
Once a Mouse by Brown, Scribners.
Petunia by Duvoisin, Knopf.
Play with Me by Ets, Scholastic Book Services.
Frog Went A-Courtin' by Rojankovsky, Harcourt, Brace, Jovanovich.
The Happy Lion by Fatio, Whittlesey House.

Dear Parents,

Can you help us? We will be setting up a Puppet Center in our classroom. Children will use the center as part of our class reading program. As children finish reading a book, they will have the chance to transform the storybook characters into puppets and share them with the class in puppet productions. Children will be planning their own puppet shows and making their own scenery and props for their performances.

We will be needing many supplies for the center. If you can contribute any of the following items, please send them to school with your child. They will greatly be appreciated by the children and certainly will help to enhance our puppet productions.

Thank you for your support and interest.

Items we can use for making puppets:

socks	paper plates
boxes	wooden spoons
gloves	felt squares
paper bags	clothespins
styrofoam balls	corks
rubber balls	Popsicle sticks

Items for trimming puppets we can use:

wallpaper scraps	fabric scraps
carpet scraps	buttons
yarn	thread
pipe cleaners	ricrac
lace	sequins
seeds	noodles
straws	cotton
feathers	ribbons

MAKE A PUPPET

Tube Puppet

Cut a construction paper face. Glue it to a paper towel tube. Add other features.

Finger Puppets

Draw faces with a water-color felt-tip pen. A handkerchief or Kleenex may be draped over your hand.

Cork Puppets

Glue a cork to a "spring-type" clothespin. Add features by gluing felt scraps and paper scraps to the cork.

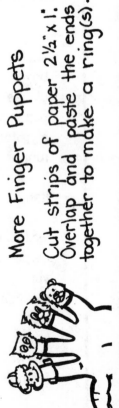

Paper Bag Puppet

Draw or paint the face on the folded end of a closed paper bag. The mouth may be drawn on the upper and bottom lip of the bag.

Spoon Puppets

Draw face features with a felt-tipped pen. Add trims with
* paper bits
* yarn
* ribbon

More Finger Puppets

Cut strips of paper 2½" x 1". Overlap and paste the ends together to make a ring(s).

Add other features with felt markers.

Paper Plate Puppet

Draw a face on a paper plate. Add other features and glue on. Glue the plate to a stick or tube.

Sock Puppets

Sew felt, material and/or yarn scraps to a sock. Buttons, ribbon and fabric scraps may also be added.

Felt Puppet

Stitch around two felt puppet shapes (leave the bottom open). "Dress" your puppet with ribbons, buttons, yarn, lace and material scraps. Stitch a mouth and add button eyes and yarn hair.

Cut out circles the size of quarters. Draw faces in each. Glue them to the rings.

Box Puppets

Paint a face onto a box. Cut out a space for the nose and mouth. Trim the puppet with...

* fabric scraps
* buttons
* yarn, ribbons
* pipe cleaners

Stick Puppets

Glue character faces to Popsicle sticks or straws. Faces may be made from construction paper.

Styrofoam Puppet

Cut a hole inside the ball large enough for your finger. Add a face with paint or marking pen. Drape material over the hand. Cut two holes for your thumb and middle finger.

PUPPET PLAY

Director

_____

PRODUCTION SCHEDULE:

Materials_____

_____

Scenery_____

_____

Crew_____

_____

Rehearsals_____

_____

Performance Date_____

_____

Title_____

_____

Author_____

MASKS AND THINGS...

Dramatization is a natural avenue for children's creative expression. It's also such an enjoyable way to make literature come alive for children. Telling a story with body movements can use many forms, from spontaneous impromptu acting with little or no costumes, to formal and prepared performances complete with background scenery, props and costumes. Whichever method you choose, you can be assured that it will be a memorable learning tool, as well as a marvelous way of exploring literature.

Children can plan their own performances if supplies and ideas are available to them. Story characters may be transformed into real-life performers by providing a few of the following materials at a center:

For making costumes:
ice-cream cartons
large bags
boxes
paper plates
cardboard
tagboard
fabric scraps
papier mache
hats

For trimming costumes:
feathers
lace, ricrac
ribbons, yarn, string
crepe and tissue paper
spools
tin cans and jar lids
marking pens
paint, crayons
tinfoil
noodles, cotton
buttons
egg carton pieces

THE PLAY

Director _____

Title _____

Staff _____

_____

_____

Scenery _____

_____

_____

Props _____

_____

_____

_____

Rehearsals _____

_____

_____

Performance _____

5: BOOKS OR BUST!

How to set up a complete center based on a favorite classroom book.

Pioneer Days   Pioneer Fact Sheet
Teacher Checklist   Pioneer Report Award
My Contract   Box Dioramas
Ballad of Davy Crockett   ABC Pioneer List

PIONEER DAYS

PIONEER DAYS
OX-CART MAN
DANIEL BOONE

MILK
MILK CARTONS

IDEA: How 'bout a Pioneer Day? Each child can come dressed as a pioneer he has read about.

OX-CART MAN

There are hundreds of books just ideal for making science and social studies themes come to life. The pictures and vocabulary are rich with ideas to elaborate on in class. *Ox-Cart Man* by Donald Hall is just one of those books.

Objectives

This center is designed to use activities elaborating on the "pioneer theme" in the Caldecott winner, *Ox-Cart Man*. Children will have the opportunity of focusing on this theme in depth, as well as elaborating on the vocabulary and ideas used in the book.

Center Display

Provide an attractive display of pioneer symbols under a colorful bulletin board. Children can help you to gather such things as quilts, candles, corn, spinning wheels, butter churns, pottery, rocking chairs, horseshoes, tools and other items from the pioneer past. Books about the era as well as pictures can also be attractive additions.

Bulletin Board

Have the children sponge paint a sky background on white butcher paper. Cotton clouds, construction paper pine trees, flowers and small forest animals may be added to the background. As children complete their log cabin writing books, they may be added to the display. Cutout letters with a saying such as "Pioneer Days" may be pinned up as a final touch.

Pioneer Scene

As children complete their covered wagons and log cabins on their contracts, they may be added to a large classroom scene. Children may begin by sponge painting green grass to a large piece of cardboard. Easter basket green grass may also be added. Animals, trees, and additional frontier village buildings may be added to the display.

Contracts

Children may do the center tasks in any order. As a child completes a task and is checked off by the teacher, he may color in the number corresponding to the task he completed.

TEACHER CHECKLIST

Theme: _Pioneer Days_

Objectives: _To familiarize children with pioneer days, particularly: pioneer heroes, survival methods, life-styles, Pony Express, living conditions, crafts, ways of life, food._

Bulletin Board and Displays: _1) background: sponge paint blue sky; green mtns; add pine tree cutouts; forest animals; log cabin books._
(2) 3D scene: milk carton wagons and log cabins; children can make flat boats; sponge pinetrees; pipecleaner pioneer people.

Books:
Daniel Boone; Daugherty
Buffalo Bill; d'Aulaire
First Wagons to Calif; Chester
Abe Lincoln; d'Aulaire
Ox-Cart Man; Hall
Johnny Cake Ho!

Songs, Poems, Records:
Davy Crockett
O'Susanna

Special Project Ideas: (art, drama, projects): _make candles; quilts; braided rugs_
bake bread, johnny cakes, pumpkin pie
Buffalo stew, corn pudding
Turn class into pioneer village - jail;
schoolhouse, livery stable, general store

Special Activities: (films, speakers, field trips): _visit "Frontier Village_
watch "Little House on the Prairie."

Work Sheets/Learning Materials: _survival worksheet._
do crossword puzzle or Ox-Cart Man
word searches - pioneer words
Ballad of Davy Crockett; (record player)

My Contract

by _____

1 Read the book, <u>Ox-Cart Man</u> or another book about the pioneers.

2 You need: [paper] [scissors] [glue] [pencil] [yarn]

Make a log-cabin cover for your writing book. Copy the sample at the center.

3 Listen carefully to the 🔘 of Davy Crockett.

What was the song about?
Write your answer on the song sheet.

4 You need: [milk carton] [scissors] [record] [glue] [paint] [paper]

Make a milk carton-covered wagon. Paint it. Write a story about it in your book. Where does it go?

5 Find out about a famous pioneer American. Write down what you discovered on the Pioneer Fact Sheet.

6 You need: [milk] [glue] [paper] [scissors] [pretzels] pretzels.

Make a log cabin out of pretzels. Make the roof from paper.

MATERIALS for PIONEER CONTRACT

Provide a Pioneer Days Contract for each child.

Provide copies of the book, *Ox-Cart Man* by Donald Hall (Viking Press).

For nonreading students, you may tape-record the story. Students may follow along as they listen.

Provide a sample of the log cabin book cover at the center. Have available the following items for each student's booklet:

1 9" x 12" brown piece of construction paper to glue the "logs" onto
2 white 3" x 3" square papers for the windows
7 12" x 4" dark brown construction paper strips to roll up as "logs"
1 15" x 4" light brown paper strip for the roof
1 12"x 12" brown piece of construction paper to serve as the back cover of the book
writing paper to staple inside the booklet
glue, scissors and pencils

Form the 12" x 4" brown paper strips into logs by rolling them around a pencil and pasting them down along the outside edges. Glue each log next to each other. Cut the two ends of the 15" x 4" strip diagonally for the roof and glue it to the top of the paper. Add two white windows on the logs. Curtains and window panes may be added with crayon. A chimney or door may also be added with construction paper strips. Staple the writing pages inside the book cover for the finished product. Children may use the book to write their finished pioneer reports inside of or to write a fictional story about pioneer days.

Provide a copy of the record "Ballad of Davy Crockett" by Tom Blackburn and George Bruns, a record player (or tape recorder) and earphones. Duplicate an adequate number of pages of the "Ballad of Davy Crockett" work sheet. Children will listen to the lyrics and write a description of what they heard on the work sheet.

Each child will need a small milk carton (or shoe box) for the activity. Cut off the top diagonal section of the carton. Children may paint the wagon section of their cartons with brown paint that has been mixed with a small amount of detergent. Paint will then adhere to the carton. Wheels may be added by gluing small bottle caps to the sides of the wagon or by fastening circular cardboard shapes with brads to the carton. Glue a white strip of construction paper to the two sides, leaving a height of at least three inches and each of the two ends open. Oxen or horses may be made out of clay, pipe cleaners or cardboard. The covered wagons may be added to the Pioneer Scene display.

Each child can choose a famous American pioneer or pioneer event for his Pioneer Report. A few ideas appear below. Duplicate an adequate number of work sheets for each child. The final report may be written in the log cabin shape book. Oral reports may also be given. A Pioneer Report Award may also be given to each child. Duplicate an award on bright-colored construction paper for each child.
A few ideas for reports can include:

William (Buffalo Bill) Cody	Davy Crockett
General Custer	Daniel Boone
Lewis and Clark	Kit Carson
Calamity Jane	Marcus Whitman
Sitting Bull	Mark Twain
Abraham Lincoln	Santa Fe
Andrew Jackson	Pony Express
Overland Stage	Fort McPherson
Virginia City	Jesse James

The children will need small milk cartons for the activity. Cartons may be painted brown by adding a small amount of detergent to the paint. To make the cartons have a "log cabin" look, children may glue pretzels, small twigs, matchsticks or toothpicks along the sides of the cartons. Windows can be cut out or painted white. Small cloth curtains may be added. Doors may be cut at the top and on one side so they swing out or just marked with pen. The roofs may be depicted by gluing Popsicle sticks on top diagonally or by stapling pieces of brown construction paper to the tops. Add the log cabins to the Pioneer Scene. Children can also make small pioneer people, gardens, trees and animals out of some of the materials mentioned on the Diorama pages in this section.

Ballad of Davy Crockett

1. Listen carefully to the words in the "Ballad of Davy Crockett."

2. Write a few sentences below telling what the song is about.

_____

_____

_____

_____

_____

_____

_____

_____

_____

_____

_____

_____

3. Draw a picture on the back of this page about the song.

Listener _____

PIONEER FACT SHEET
by_____

The pioneer person or event I will study is:

_____

List at least 3 facts you want to find out

_____

_____

_____

List 3 books you will use to find your facts.

_____

_____

_____

The date I will turn my report in is:

_____

Teacher Signature:

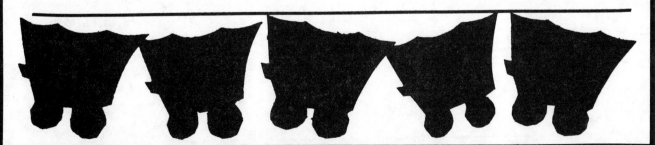

DIORAMAS

Dioramas can be an especially fun project to elaborate on a favorite book that has been read. A diorama portrays an idea in three-dimensional form. The possibilities for scenes are endless!

BOX DIORAMA

Box dioramas, as the name suggests, begin with a box. A shoe box will serve nicely for an individual diorama. Larger projects may need to be housed within larger-sized boxes. Any sturdy box will do. The open side becomes the front where the scene is viewed. The top of the box may be open or closed. The background (the inside of the back of the box) can be painted, decorated with cutouts or covered with wallpaper or gift-wrapping paper. Be sure to extend this decoration onto the sides, also.

DECORATIONS

Children will enjoy thinking up how to depict their miniature scenes. Just provide a host of properties and watch their imaginations work! When given the opportunity, children usually can come up with creative ways to represent the animals, people, buildings or plants needed. A few ideas to get you started, though, are:

ROCKS
small pebbles
large gravel
chunks of painted sponge

SNOW
cotton batting
styrofoam
detergent beaten with a little water until it's stiff

FENCES
small twigs
toothpicks
soda straws
all may be held in place with clay

TREES

small pine cones painted green
cotton or sponge dipped in green paint
small branches held in bits of clay or spools
construction-paper cutouts
green clay
cardboard covered with bark

FLOWERS

crepe paper, tissue, cloth or colored construction paper cut in small circular bits and fluffed up
bits of colored clay

BUILDINGS

Small boxes, such as milk cartons, serve nicely for houses. Milk cartons may be covered with paper or painted by mixing a little detergent into the paint. It will then adhere to the carton. Add details by gluing on some of the following:

    pretzels
    Popsicle sticks
    sugar cubes
    small pebbles
    corrugated cardboard
    small twigs
    heavy sandpaper
    matchsticks
    soda straws

Windows can be cut out or painted white. Small cloth curtains may be added. Doors may be cut at the top and on one side so they swing out or just marked with pen. The roof may be depicted with Popsicle sticks glued on top or construction paper stapled to the top.

ANIMALS AND PEOPLE

A few of the following ideas may be used to represent animals or people:

    corks
    clay
    cardboard tubes
    pipe cleaners
    felt-tipped-pen drawn onto construction paper or cardboard
    magazine cutouts
    variety store figures
    clothespins
    spools

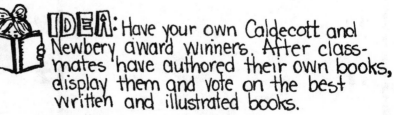

IDEA: Have your own Caldecott and Newbery award winners. After classmates have authored their own books, display them and vote on the best written and illustrated books.

ABC PIONEER LIST
by _____

There are many things that the pioneer people used during the frontier days. Can you think of a "pioneer thing" for each letter of the alphabet? If you get stumped, try to think of an animal, tool, type of food or clothing for the letter.

a

b

c

d

e

f

g

h

i

j

k

l

m

n

o

p

q

r

s

t

u

v

w

x

y

z

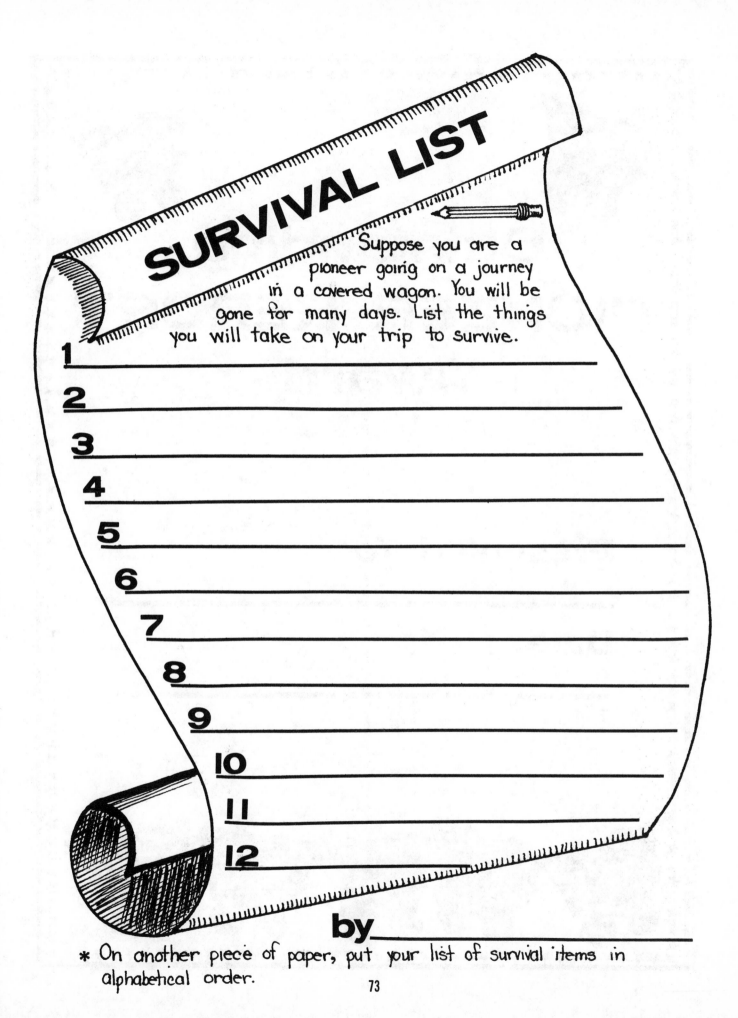

SURVIVAL LIST

Suppose you are a pioneer going on a journey in a covered wagon. You will be gone for many days. List the things you will take on your trip to survive.

1 _____
2 _____
3 _____
4 _____
5 _____
6 _____
7 _____
8 _____
9 _____
10 _____
11 _____
12 _____

by_____

* On another piece of paper, put your list of survival items in alphabetical order.

73

Outstanding
PIONEER REPORT
Award

Presented To:

_____

Date:

_____

6: BOOK FLINGS

Book centers, contracts, activities and ideas to make science concepts meaningful to children.

Trees
Frogs and Toads
Islands
Snow
Winter
Fog

Measurement
Ocean Life
Owls
Wind
Beauty of Nature
Shadows

THE CENTER

In this section, children will have a chance to explore authors' words through creative experiences. Books have been specifically chosen to stimulate children's imaginations and to heighten their sensitivities toward living things and the natural world. You may use the selection mentioned or another appropriate book. There are many to choose from.

SETTING UP THE CENTER

Although it is not necessary to use a learning center for these activities, a sample center has been pictured for you. The center should be set up in the room in a corner convenient to the flow of traffic. At the center, children will be able to find the materials necessary for completing their contracts. The center may include a bulletin board where children's work may be displayed. Contracts, patterns and sample activities may also be hung for reference.

A list of supplies needed for each contract is included on the Material Sheets listed in this section. In addition, you may wish to include these supplies on a permanent basis at the center:

> copies of the book
> pencils
> crayons
> glue/paste
> writing paper
> construction paper
> scissors
> a tape recorder and earphones
> (for any children in your room
> who are unable to read the book)

CONTRACTS

Duplicate a copy of the contract for each child and have the copies available at the center. Activities on the contract may be done as a group, small group or individual basis. As each activity is completed, the child may color in the designated space on the contract.

NOTE: The introductory section of this book contains a page of directions for setting up learning centers.

A Tree Is Nice

IDEA: How 'bout a Book Sharing Month. Each day a different student can bring a favorite book from home to read or have read.

A TREE IS NICE

Name **Date**

 Read <u>A Tree Is Nice</u> by Janice May Udry. or another story about trees.

1

Look carefully at all the leaves in the folder. Sort the leaves into groups that are alike. Can you think of a different way? Examine your leaves.

2

 Choose three different kinds of leaves. Can you find the leaves in the leaf book? What kinds of trees do the leaves come from? Write the names down.

3

Leaf Mountings
Arrange your labeled leaves between two pieces of wax paper. Have the teacher help you press over the papers with a warm iron. Include the names of the leaves.

4

 Trace around the leaf pattern. Cut them out. On each leaf write a different reason why you think trees are nice. Tie the leaves to your branch. Hang up your leaf mobile.

5

Materials

Provide copies of the book *A Tree Is Nice* by Janice May Udry, Harper & Row, or any other appropriate story. If you have children unable to read the book, you can tape the story on a cassette.

Children will arrange their labeled leaves between two pieces of wax paper (leaves must be fresh). At a separate location, an adult can help to press the leaves between the paper with a warm iron. Attractive frames may be made by gluing strips of construction paper or plastic tape around the mounting. The mountings may also be made to look like scrolls by gluing a strip of black construction paper on the top and bottom of the wax paper.

Children will help you bring in small branches for the leaf project. Provide several tagboard leaf patterns for children to trace around. Red, yellow, green, orange and brown construction paper should be available for tracing the leaf patterns onto. The patterns are then cut out. On the patterns children write reasons why they think trees are nice. Several leaves should be used by each child. The leaves are punched with a paper punch near the top of each pattern and tied to the branch with string or yarn. The mobiles may be hung from the classroom ceiling.

Children can help you to gather different kinds of leaves. These may be displayed at the center. Provide several magnifying glasses for children to examine their leaves with. As a follow-up activity, children can draw or write how they sorted their leaf groups.

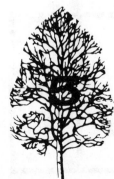

Provide several reference books about leaves and trees at the center. You may wish to first show children how they can use the books in locating the names of the leaves at the center. Provide writing paper or a ditto for children to write their answers on.

FROG AND TOAD TOGETHER

Name _____ **Date** _____

Read the book <u>Frog and Toad Together</u> by Arnold Lobel or another book about frogs.

1

Frog Books

1. Trace around the frog pattern on two pieces of green construction paper.
2. Cut the shape out.
3. Staple several pieces of writing paper inside the shape.

2

Write your own frog and toad story. What friendly thing will they do for each other?
Write your story in the shape book.

3

Find out about frogs and toads.
   What do they eat?
   Where do they live?
   How do they catch their food?
   How are they alike?
   How are they different?
Write the answers in your shape book.

4

Poems
   Make a list of words that rhyme with "frog" and "toad" in your book. Now make up a silly poem about a frog and a toad.

Frog
log
smog

toad
load
road

5

Materials

 Provide copies of the book *Frog and Toad Together* by Arnold Lobel, Harper. For children who are unable to read the book, you can tape the story on a cassette.

 Duplicate an adequate number of pages of the frog shape for student booklets. If possible, use green paper for the cover of the booklet. If you do not wish to make a stencil of the frog, tagboard patterns may also be provided for children to trace around. Several pieces of writing paper are stapled inside the shape book. Have scissors, pencils, crayons and a stapler available.

 Provide scratch paper for story drafts. Children may also enjoy reading *Frog and Toad* by Arnold Lobel, Harper, for additional story ideas.

4 Provide several reference books and filmstrips about frogs and toads. Children can find out about the animals in the books and write their findings in their shape books. Children may also observe real frogs and toads that have been brought in from home.

 Children will make lists of rhyming words that rhyme with "frog" and "toad" in their shape books. Words rhyming with "frog" can include dog, log, bog, hog and smog. Words rhyming with "toad" can include load and road. Children can make up silly poems about a frog and a toad and write them in their books.

THE LITTLE ISLAND

Name   **Date**

Read the book <u>The Little Island</u> by Golden MacDonald or another book about islands.

1

Pretend you're shipwrecked on an island. Write a message on a strip of paper. Write on it where you are and what happened. How will people find you?

2

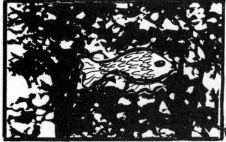

Blot a piece of white construction paper with a sponge dipped in blue paint. Cut underwater sea life out of construction paper, and glue them onto the scene.

3

What is an island?
Name some other islands.
Locate them on a map.
What is the largest island in the world? Where is it?

4

Find out about a special island. Why would you want to go there? Paint a travel poster telling others about your island.

5

Materials

1 Provide copies of the book *The Little Island* by Golden MacDonald. For children who are unable to read the book, you can tape the story on a cassette.

2 Provide strips of butcher paper cut into lengths of 3" x 15" for each child. Children write messages on the paper and then wind them up and store them in top of old glass bottles. (They can then be easily removed.) Messages can look aged by slightly tearing each side of the paper along the edges and wrinkling the page in your hand.

3 White construction paper (12" x 18") will be needed for each child. Also provide blue paint in tin plates and sponges that have been cut into small pieces. Sponges will be used as paintbrushes by dipping the sponge into the paint and then pressing down and lifting up on the white paper. Underwater sea life and animals may be made by cutting figures from scraps of construction paper and gluing them to the painted construction paper.

4 Provide several reference books, encyclopedias and filmstrips about islands. Writing paper should also be available for each child. Maps may also be provided for children to look up famous islands on.

5 Provide travel posters and brochures available from travel companies. A variety of colored construction paper or poster board will also be needed. Paint, watercolor pens, colored pencils, crayons, scissors, construction paper and glue may be provided at the center.

THE SNOWY DAY

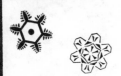 

Name   **Date**

Read the book <u>The Snowy Day</u> by Ezra Jack Keats or another book about snow.

1

 Study the artwork of Ezra Jack Keats. Find a picture you like in the book. Try to make one just like it. Cut the figures out of construction paper. Glue them to a snowy background.

2

 Make a snowflake!

   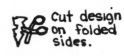

1. Cut a circle   Fold in 1/2   2. fold again in thirds   Fold 1/3 in half again   Cut design on folded sides.

Open and say, "ah-h-h!"

3

Write the word "snow" in the middle of your snowflake. How many words can you think of to rhyme with your word? Write them. Can you make up a "snowy poem" using the words?

4

Find out about snow. What causes snow?

5

Materials

Provide copies of the book *The Snowy Day* by Ezra Jack Keats, Viking. For children who are unable to read the book, you can tape the story on a cassette or copies of the record are available from Weston Woods.

Provide several copies of Ezra Jack Keats' artwork such as *The Snowy Day, Whistle for Willie, In a Spring Garden, Jennie's Hat, Goggles* and *Hi, Cat!* Children can study the similarities of Keats' work in the books. Provide white construction paper, colored construction paper scraps, glue, scissors and pencils. Children can make their own collages on the white construction paper.

Have available lightweight paper for snowflakes and scissors. Children can cut snowflakes to decorate the classroom windows by following a pattern you have provided or the description on their contracts.

Provide pencils and scratch paper for poem drafts. Children write rhyming words to the word "snow" on one of their snowflakes. They may use these words to help them create a "snowy poem." Finished poems may be written on writing paper and pinned to bulletin boards with the cutout snowflakes framing them.

Provide several reference books and filmstrips about snow. Each child can discover snow in these books. A shape book may be made for each child to write his discoveries in. Provide two sheets of blue construction paper for the cover of the book. Writing paper may be stapled inside the cover. A snowflake may be pasted on the cover of the book, and then each child may cut his book into the shape of the snowflake outline.

WHITE SNOW, BRIGHT SNOW

Name _____ **Date** _____

1
Read the book <u>White Snow, Bright Snow</u> by Alvin Tresselt or another book about snow.

2
SNOWY PICTURE
Make a snowy scene on black paper. Dip a pencil point (for thin dots) or pencil eraser (for thicker dots) into white paint. Press down and pick up for each dot.

You need: white paint, pencil, black paper

3
Look up the weather forecast for the day. What part of the U.S. has snow?
Fill in a U.S. map. Color in all the snowy areas.

THE DAILY NEWS

4
SNOWY WORDS
"White" and "bright" are two words that describe snow. How many more can you think of? Write them. How would it...
... taste?   ... smell?   ... sound?
... feel?   ... look?

ADJECTIVES
White
bright

5

MACARONI SNOWFLAKES
Spread a piece of wax paper on a table. Make a lacy snowflake by sticking noodles together with glue. Let your snowflake dry for a few hours. Hang it up.

WAX PAPER

Materials

Provide copies of the book *White Snow, Bright Snow* by Alvin Tresselt, published by Lothrop. For children who are unable to read the book, you can tape the story on a cassette.

Provide black construction paper (9" x 12" or 12" x 18") and a pencil with an eraser for each child (these may also be furnished from home by the children). Thick, white paint may be placed in margarine tubs or pie tins for easy accessibility. Children depict a snowy scene by using the ends of their pencils. Larger dots may be made by dipping the eraser end in the paint and pressing down on the black paper. Smaller dots are made by dipping the pencil point in the paint. In order for the scene to show up, dots should be placed closely together.

Provide a ditto of a United States map. Children may bring in the weather forecast from newspapers or listen to the news on a radio or television station. They may then depict the snowy areas of the U.S. by coloring in their maps accordingly.

Provide scratch paper for the children. Each child may make a list of his or her own words that describe snow. These words may then be added to a permanent list supplied by compiling the words all the children have come up with.

Provide wax paper, glue, toothpicks, yarn or string and various kinds of noodles. Children make their macaroni snowflakes by working on sheets of wax paper and gluing pieces of macaroni together. Each piece must touch another piece. Finished products may be hung from the ceiling or windows.

HIDE AND SEEK FOG

Name _____ **Date** _____

Read <u>Hide</u> <u>and</u> <u>Seek</u> <u>Fog</u> by Alvin Tresselt. or another book about fog.	**1**

You need:

Make a foggy scene. Paste black and brown construction paper cut-outs onto a gray construction paper background. Glue a layer of wax paper over the scene.

2

Foggy Stories

Pretend you are on a ship at sea.
Fog begins to roll in. It's hard to see.
Tell what happens.
How do you make it to shore (or do you)?

A foggy day.

3

U.S. FORECAST

DATA SUPPLIED BY NATIONAL WEATHER SERVICE FOR FRIDAY, SEPTEMBER 26, 1980

Find a U.S. weather forecast. What is the symbol for fog? What parts of the country are foggy?

Fill in a U.S. map. Color in all the foggy areas.

4

Research
What is fog?
What is it made of?
What causes it?

5

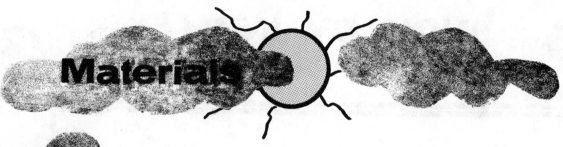

Materials

Provide copies of *Hide and Seek Fog* by Alvin Tresselt published by Lothrop. For children who are unable to read the book, you can tape the story on a cassette.

Provide a sheet of gray construction paper 12" x 18" for each child. Smaller sheets of black and brown construction paper, as well as a sheet of wax paper (12" x 18"), should also be available for each child. Scissors and glue should be accessible.

Children will write "foggy stories" on writing paper. Preceding the writing task, a discussion concerning the hazards of fog at sea or on the road may help to provide writing ideas for children.

Provide a ditto of a United States map. Children may bring in the weather forecast from newspapers or listen to the news on a radio or television station. They may then depict the foggy areas of the U.S. by coloring in their maps accordingly.

Provide several reference books or filmstrips on fog. Children can research the topic and write their findings on writing paper. Findings may also be presented orally in reports.

INCH BY INCH

Name   **Date**

1

Read the book <u>Inch</u> <u>by</u> <u>Inch</u> by Leo Lionni or another book about measurement.

2

You need: ball of string   scissors   labels   yardstick   tape

1. Cut string lengths for each of the body parts.
2. Measure each body part. How many inches is it?
3. Write the answer on each label. Tape it to the string.

neck   head   hand   foot   arm

3

FIND IT!   Find something in the room that is about...

3 inches long _____.
12 inches long _____.
24 inches long _____.
36 inches long _____.
(Write your answers on the lines above.)

4

How long is...

a pencil _____   a paper_____

scissors_____   a crayon_____

5

How long are you?   Use a tape measure. and a friend.

I am ☐ inches tall.

My friend is ☐ inches.

90

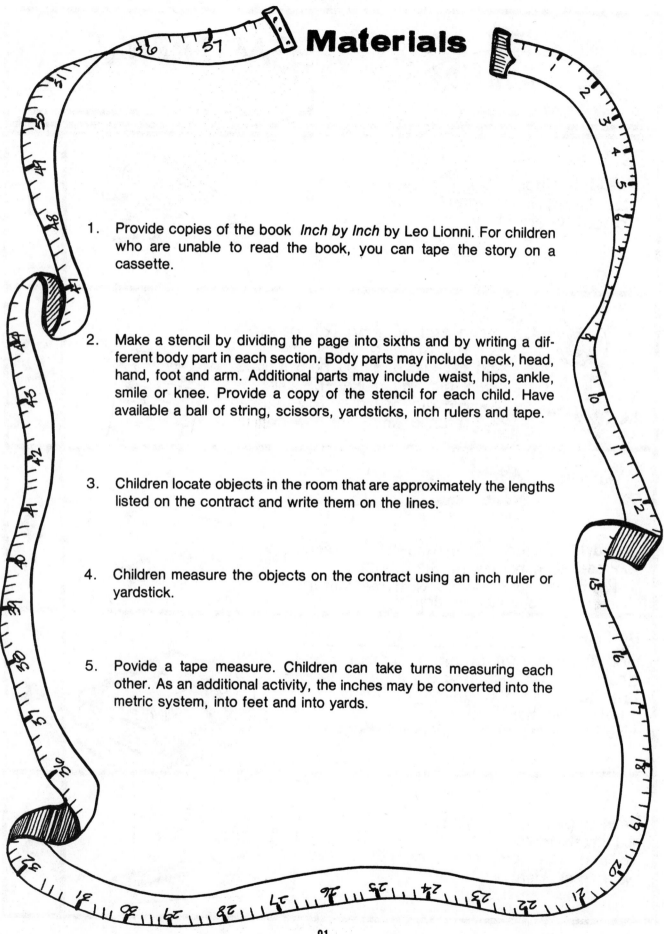

Materials

1. Provide copies of the book *Inch by Inch* by Leo Lionni. For children who are unable to read the book, you can tape the story on a cassette.

2. Make a stencil by dividing the page into sixths and by writing a different body part in each section. Body parts may include neck, head, hand, foot and arm. Additional parts may include waist, hips, ankle, smile or knee. Provide a copy of the stencil for each child. Have available a ball of string, scissors, yardsticks, inch rulers and tape.

3. Children locate objects in the room that are approximately the lengths listed on the contract and write them on the lines.

4. Children measure the objects on the contract using an inch ruler or yardstick.

5. Povide a tape measure. Children can take turns measuring each other. As an additional activity, the inches may be converted into the metric system, into feet and into yards.

SWIMMY

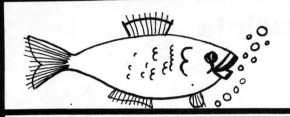

by_____

Read the book <u>Swimmy</u> by Leo Lionni or another book about ocean life.

1

Pretend you are an ocean diver. Write a story about an exciting dive you have made. Why did you make the dive? Where did the dive take place? Describe what you saw and did.

2

You need:

paint   crayons   paper

Draw a picture of an underwater scene. Press down hard with the crayons. Paint over your picture with the water paint. Let your picture dry.

3

My fish is _____.
Find information about a special fish.
What does he look like?
How large is the animal?
What does the fish eat?
Use at least three different books.

4

Draw a picture of the fish you chose to report on. Color it the same colors as your real fish.

5

Materials

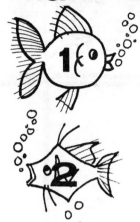

Provide copies of the book *Swimmy* by Leo Lionni, Pantheon Books. For children who are unable to read the book, you can tape the story on a cassette.

Children are to write underwater stories about pretend dives they have made. Provide writing paper and pencils for them. You may wish to motivate the writing activity through pictures and stories of real ocean diving expeditions. Perhaps a parent or class friend who is an ocean diver can visit the classroom and bring in his or her underwater diving equipment to share.

Provide white drawing paper for each child 12" x 18". Pictures of underwater sea life may be placed at the center as references for children. Children will draw underwater scenes using their crayons. Emphasize to the class the importance of pressing down with the crayons and to color in the drawings they have made. When children have completed their drawings, they lightly paint over the paper with a paint wash supplied at the center. To make the paint wash, place about one tablespoon of blue paint into a quart jar and fill the remainder of the jar with water. Mix the mixture thoroughly.

Children will study underwater fish (or sea animals) of their choice. Provide several books on sea life at your class library for children to use as references. Children should try and discover as much as they can about their fish. Their findings may either be written in report form or given orally to the class.

Children will draw pictures of their fish that they reported on. Crayons, pen and ink, paint, or cut-and-paste paper scraps are a few of the mediums children may choose from. The pictures should be realistic representations of their fish. Reference books from home or school should be used as a guide to the color of their fish.

THE HAPPY OWLS

by_____

1
Read the book _The Happy Owls_ by Celestino Piatti or another book about owls.

2
Make a "sunflower of happiness." On each petal write something that makes you feel happy.

3
1. Fold your paper into 4 parts.
2. Write the name of a season in each box.
3. Draw a picture to show something that happened to the owls for each season.

Fall | Winter

Spring | Summer

4
You need:

Make an owl shape book. Staple writing paper inside. Color your cover.

5
Read about owls. Find out 5 interesting facts about them. Write these facts in your owl shape book.

MATERIALS

① Provide copies of the book *The Happy Owls* by Celestino Piatti, Atheneum Publishers. For children who are unable to read the book, you can tape the story on a cassette. The record of the story is available through Weston Woods.

② Children will make their own "sunflowers of happiness" like the kind that appeared in the story. Each child can make his own sunflower center by tracing around a coffee can (or similar size circular shape) onto an 8½" x 11" piece of yellow construction paper. Flower petals may be made by having the children trace around tagboard petal patterns that you have provided. Children will write things that make them feel happy on petals and attach to the flower centers with paste.

③ Provide 12" x 18" drawing paper for each child. Children will fold the paper into fourths and then write the name of each season at the top of one of the boxes. You may wish to provide a pattern for the children to copy at a center. Children will then depict each season as it appeared in the story by drawing a picture in the box. Spring, for instance, could be represented by trees, with buds and leaves, meadows covered with tiny flowers and birds. These were mentioned by the owls in their story to the barnyard friends.

④ Provide a tagboard pattern of a "roundish oval" to represent the body of the owl. Children may trace this onto precut light brown (9" x 12") pieces of construction paper. Two oval shapes should be cut out by each child to represent the front and back of the owl shape book. The top of the owl's head and ears is made by folding a dark brown piece of construction paper 7" x 7" into a triangular shape. Eyes may be made by tracing around two 3" circles onto yellow construction paper. Smaller black circles cut from black paper may be added as the center of the eyes. A small orange square folded in two serves as the owl's beak. The owl features are then pasted onto the light brown owl shape. Feathers may be drawn with black crayons. Pages may then be added inside the shape book cover and "cut to shape." Staple the pages between the cover at the top of the book.

⑤ Each child will find five interesting facts out about owls. You may wish to provide several reference books about owls at your class library. Children may elaborate about these facts in the owl shape book.

GILBERTO AND THE WIND

Name   **Date**

 Read the book <u>Gilberto and the Wind</u> by Marie Hall Ets, (Viking Press)or another book about wind.  **1**

 Pretend you are a kite flying high in the sky. The wind is pushing you gently along. What do you see and where do you go?
Write your story.  **2**

You need:

windy | still
a paper folded in half.

1. Look carefully at the pictures in the book.

2. How did the person who drew the pictures (the illustrator) show that it was a "windy day?" Draw a picture on one side to show a "windy day." On the other side draw a picture to show a "still day."  **3**

Find out information about wind.
What causes it?
What is a tornado?
What is "wind at the sea" called?  **4**

Make your own kite.

1. Draw around pattern.

2. Cut it out.

3. Use crayons to draw a face on the kite.

4. Cut a piece of yarn as long as your arm.

5. Staple the yarn to the bottom of the kite face.

6. Cut pieces of crepe paper.

7. Twist the crepe paper around the yarn to make bows. **5**

Materials

Provide copies of the book *Gilberto and the Wind* by Marie Hall Ets, Viking Press. The record is also available if you have children unable to read the book (Weston Woods), or you can tape the story on a cassette.

Children may either write their responses (or dictate them to you) on separate pieces of paper for each task, or you may wish to have them make their own "Wind Journals." "Wind Journals" may be made in the shape of a kite with a variety of colored construction paper (11" x 9") covers. Several sheets of writing paper may then be stapled inside each cover and cut in the same kite shape. Children may then decorate the covers of their "Wind Journals" following the directions on Task 5.

Children will use *Gilberto and the Wind* to observe how artists portray windy days (wavy lines). Perhaps they can also discover this in other classroom books. Children may then draw their discoveries either in their "Wind Journals" or on folded 12" x 18" pieces of drawing paper. On one side of the page they will depict how Marie Hall Ets represents wind in her book (wavy lines). On the opposite side of the page, children can draw the same scene without the wind (still).

Children will discover what causes wind using class, library or home reference books. These discoveries may be written or dictated in their "Wind Journals" or on separate pieces of writing paper.

Provide several kite patterns made from tagboard for the children to trace. A variety of colored construction paper, precut 11" x 9", will also be needed. Also provide crepe paper, yarn, scissors, stapler and crayons. Children then follow the directions for "How to Make a Kite" on Task 5. You may wish to hang the finished kites or "Wind Journals" on a bulletin board.

TIME OF WONDER

Name _____ **Date** _____

Read the book <u>Time of Wonder</u> by Robert McCloskey.	**1**
Make a "water shape book." Staple several pieces of writing paper inside two pieces of blue construction paper. Staple the pages. Cut "waves" along the top. Decorate your book with "things of wonder."	**2**
SAILBOATS 1. Push a thumbtack in the middle of a cork. 2. Cut a triangular-shaped sail from paper. Thread a toothpick through the sail as shown. 3. Carefully stick the sail into the cork. 4. Place corkboat in water. Does it move? How? What happens when you blow? Write what you learn in your book.	**3**
1. Outside, put a stick in the ground. Put a long strip of cloth on the stick. 2. Watch it carefully, at least 3 different times. Write what you see each time in your book. When did it blow the most? Why? 3. Watch what the wind does to trees, pieces of paper, dust, clothing. Write about it in your book.	**4**
Write the words "fall," "winter," "spring," "summer" at the top of each page in your book. Write the sights and sounds you see and hear for each season in <u>Time of Wonder</u>.	**5**

Materials

Provide copies of the book *Time of Wonder* by Robert McCloskey, Viking Press. For children who are unable to read the book, you can tape the story on a cassette.

Provide two pieces of 9" x 12" blue construction paper for each child and several pieces of writing paper for each book. Each child will use the blue paper as a cover to be stapled over several pieces of writing paper. The top of the book is cut in scallops to represent waves. An underwater scene may be depicted on the cover of the shape book using crayons or construction paper designs cut and pasted.

Provide corks, thumbtacks, toothpicks and light paper. A small bowl or tub half-filled with water should be placed on form or in a low pan to catch any water leakage. Sailboat races can be a special part of the center with the winner receiving a special award.

A long piece of cloth can be tied to a long stick and stuck in the ground outside the classroom. Children should observe the stick at least three different times a day.

Children will use four pages of their water shape books for this activity. On the top of each of the pages children write the name of a different season such as "fall," "winter," "summer," or "spring." Children will look through the book, *Time of Wonder,* and write words depicting the sights and sounds of each of the seasons on the correct page in their shape books.

COME OUT SHADOW, WHEREVER YOU ARE!

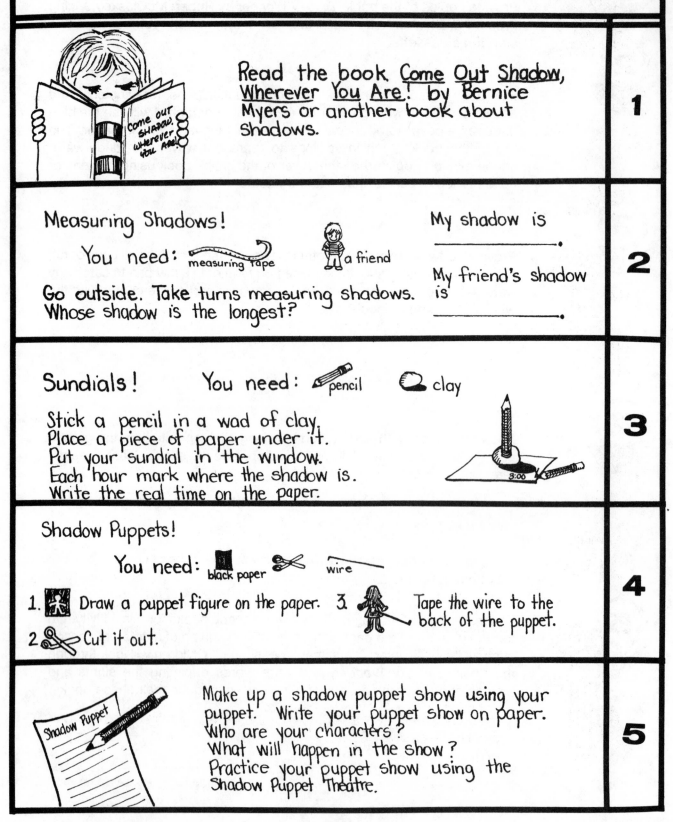

1 Read the book Come Out Shadow, Wherever You Are! by Bernice Myers or another book about shadows.

2 Measuring Shadows!

You need: measuring tape   a friend

Go outside. Take turns measuring shadows. Whose shadow is the longest?

My shadow is _____.

My friend's shadow is _____.

3 Sundials!   You need: pencil   clay

Stick a pencil in a wad of clay.
Place a piece of paper under it.
Put your sundial in the window.
Each hour mark where the shadow is.
Write the real time on the paper.

4 Shadow Puppets!

You need: black paper   wire

1. Draw a puppet figure on the paper.
2. Cut it out.
3. Tape the wire to the back of the puppet.

5 Make up a shadow puppet show using your puppet. Write your puppet show on paper.
Who are your characters?
What will happen in the show?
Practice your puppet show using the Shadow Puppet Theatre.

Materials

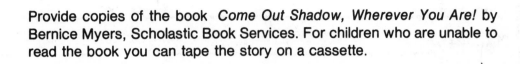

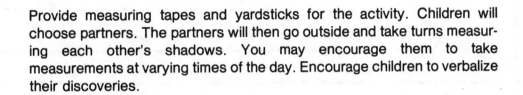

1 Provide copies of the book *Come Out Shadow, Wherever You Are!* by Bernice Myers, Scholastic Book Services. For children who are unable to read the book you can tape the story on a cassette.

2 Provide measuring tapes and yardsticks for the activity. Children will choose partners. The partners will then go outside and take turns measuring each other's shadows. You may encourage them to take measurements at varying times of the day. Encourage children to verbalize their discoveries.

3 Each child will need a pencil, a wad of clay and a piece of paper. Provide enough space near windowsills for each child to place his or her own sundial. After children have recorded the shadow placement on their papers each hour (or convenient intervals), have them analyze their papers. Children should be encouraged to verbalize or write down any discoveries they have made. Discussions can then take place concerning the reliability of sundials. Children can make comparisons of one another's measurements.

4 Shadow puppets may be made from black tagboard paper precut to 9" x 11". Enough wire for each child should be provided. Wire can be made by precutting clothes hangers. Children should then tape the wire to the back of the puppets.

A shadow puppet stage may be readily made for the class to use. Cut the bottom out of a sturdy, large grocery store box. Attach tightly drawn white cloth or paper to the cutout hole by taping the edges. Sheets or white butcher paper are handy materials to use. A lamp with the shade removed is placed behind the stage. Children then place their shadow puppets directly up against the cloth or paper.

5 Provide each child with a copy of the Shadow Puppet Work Sheet. Children may then write the puppet show ideas that they will present on the work sheets. Children can design the shows individually or together creating their own puppets and scenery from stories they have heard or originally created.

SHADOW PUPPET SHOW

Director:_____ Helpers:_____

Play Title:_____ _____

Puppets:_____

_____

Scenery:_____

_____

Tell briefly what your play is about.

_____

_____

_____

_____

_____

_____

_____

_____

_____

_____

_____

_____

_____

Teacher Approval: _____

Date of Presentation:_____

7: BOOK TRAVELS

Book centers, contracts, activities and ideas to make countries meaningful to children.

Africa

Holland

Japan

American Indians

China

Mexico

Russia

Books can open the doors to so many avenues of learning. They can also be excellent sources to help children learn about other cultures in the world. In this section, you will find many book suggestions to help children with a glimpse of different lands. You may provide the selection mentioned or another of your choice.

MATERIALS:

You may begin your study by providing an attractive display of the country. Children can help you gather such things as dolls, pottery, pictures, crafts, music and artifacts to add to the display.

You may also wish to draw on human resources - ask around for adult volunteers to share their firsthand experiences, artifacts or slides.

Duplicate enough contracts for each child to use. Children may do the center tasks in any order.

A list of materials needed to complete each contract is provided.

INSTRUMENT CHART

Guitar

You need a shoe box. Cut a hole about 3"x3" in the top lid. Wrap 5 rubber bands around the box and over the hole. Decorate the box with paint.

Drum

You need an empty oatmeal box or similar round carton. Paint and decorate. Add string with brad fasteners. Be sure to keep the top on the container.

Jangles

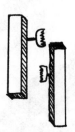

You will need a stick about 8"x ½". Flatten four bottle caps with a hammer. Attach two bottle caps, with a nail, to each stick. You may wish to paint the wood.

Xylophone

You need several pieces of hollow bamboo. Be sure each piece is a slightly different length. For the xylophone base you will need an 18-inch board and as many 4-inch nails as you have bamboo pieces. Space the nails evenly along the length of the board. Hammer them right through the board so the points stand up like spikes. Fix the bamboo pieces, in order, by pressing the solid bottom of each one over the nail and twisting it in place.

AFRICA

1 Read the book <u>Moja</u> <u>Means</u> <u>One</u> by Muriel Feelings or another book about Africa.

2 Practice reading and writing Swahili words. Make a Swahili Word Book.

3 Choose an animal to study that lives in Africa. My animal is_____.

Write down facts you learned.

4 Make an African instrument. Follow the directions on the Instrument Chart.

5 Make a fish print!

by_____

Materials

Provide a copy of the contract for each child.

Provide a copy of the book *Moja Means One* by Muriel Feelings published by Dial Press or a selection of your choice about Africa.

Make a chart of the Swahili words that appear in the book or use the words below. A few others you may wish to incorporate on your list are:

jambo - hello (JAHM-bow)   shule - school (SH OE-lay)
baba - father (BAH-bah)   tembo - elephant (TEM-bow)
mama - mother (MAH-mah)   watoto - children (wah-TOE-toe)
rofiki - friend (rah-FEE-key)   chakula - food (cah-KOO-lah)

You may wish to make a tape of the pronunciations for each word. Children can then follow along the chart and practice pronouncing the words. Each child can also make his own Swahili word book. Cut a 5½" x 8½" white page for each word. Then assemble the pages together and staple a colorful cover to the front of the book. Each page may contain a different printed word which has been appropriately illustrated.

Provide several reference books, picture charts and stuffed figures of animals native to Africa at the center. Each child can choose one animal ("tano") to study. Children may illustrate their animals by choosing any one of a number of mediums such as clay, paint, papier mache, cardboard tubes or paper.

Post the instrument ("tisa") chart on the board. Children may help by bringing the following materials from home to make their instruments:

dried bamboo in varying lengths   Any of the following to fasten onto the
nails - 4" and 2" size   dowel to make different sounds:
hammers   Tinkertoy tops
oatmeal cartons   spools
bottle caps   sponge balls
18" long board   cotton
shoe boxes   brushes
rubber bands
dowel sticks (drum beaters)

Decorating materials:
scissors   construction paper
yarn   glue/paste
crayons   sequins

Buy a medium-sized fish ("saba") with fairly large scales and fins such as sole, salmon or cod. Brush it with a water-based paint or ink. Provide each child with a sheet of rice paper or white paper. Children lay the paper over the fish and carefully smooth it down to cover the fish completely. They then rub the scales and fins with their fingers and then lift off the prints. The finished products will make lovely additions to your classroom if they are mounted with paper frames.

1. Read the book *The Cow Who Fell in the Canal* by Phyllis Krasilovsky.

2. Make a Dutch tulip.

3. Make a cow from an oatmeal box.

4. Make a Dutch village with your friends.

HOLLAND

by_____

Materials

Provide copies of *The Cow Who Fell in the Canal* by Phyllis Krasilovsky, published by Doubleday, or another selection of your choice about Holland. For children who are unable to read the book, you can tape the story on a cassette.

Provide pastel-colored plastic egg cartons, scissors, green construction paper, glue, and green pipe cleaners. You may wish to provide patterns of leaves for children to trace. Cut the bottoms of the egg cartons so that single egg cups are produced. Children cut the cups into scallops to appear like tulips. The tops of the cups are stuck with pipe cleaners. Bend the pipe cleaners in the middle of the cups so that they are secure. Leaves may be cut from green construction paper. Brush glue on one side of each leaf and wind it gently around the pipe cleaner. Several tulips may be made by each child. Attach them together with a yarn bow for tulip bouquets.

Each child will need a cylinder-shaped tube (cardboard juice cans or oatmeal boxes will do nicely or paper tubes may be used). Cover or paint the bottom and sides of the tube with white paper or paint. Tail is made by gluing a small white pipe cleaner that has been wound around a pencil to the end of the tube. Paint a face on top of the can. Black spots are painted on the body. Add paper ears and legs cut from scraps of cardboard. These may be attached by cutting slits into the box. The cow may be converted into a bank by simply cutting a slot in the top of the cow's back or by removing the top and adding pennies.

Begin making the Dutch village by collecting quart and half-gallon milk cartons several weeks before you begin the project. Study Dutch village scenes by looking at pictures. You may wish to discuss how the buildings are placed side by side. Each child may be responsible for making one house for the village. Milk carton may be painted by mixing a small amount of detergent into the colored paint. This will help the paint adhere to the surface of the container. The box may also be covered with colored construction paper. Windows and doors may be either cut out of the box (with an adult's help) or added by pasting on small square pieces of construction paper. The roof is added by folding brown construction paper over the top of the carton. Cut the ends so that they hang slightly over the carton and staple the roof onto the carton at the very top. Children can paint a large piece of butcher paper green and blue to depict the grass and the canal. Place the buildings side by side on the paper and add additional village features if desired.

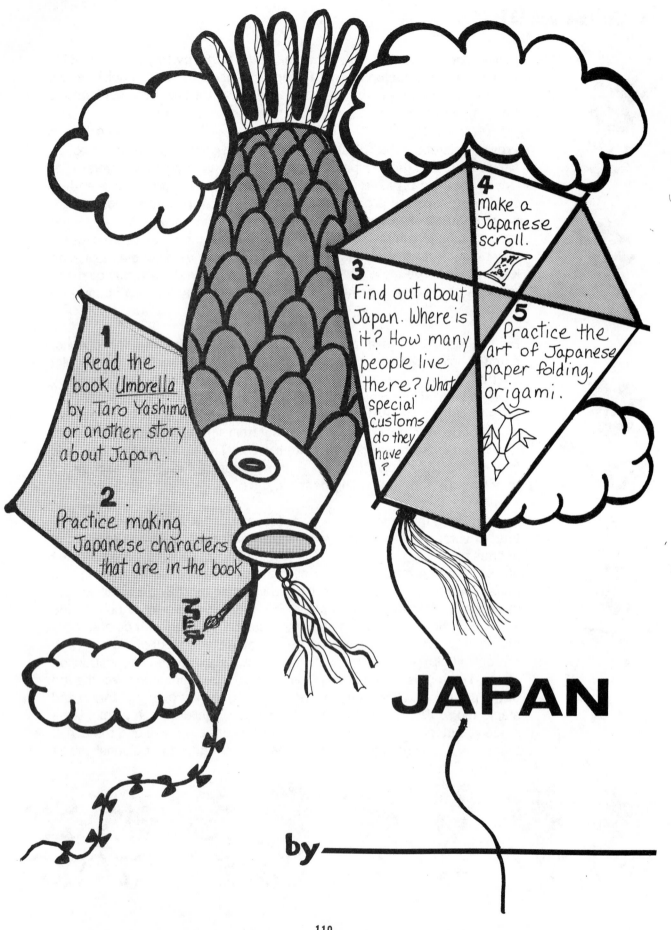

1
Read the book _Umbrella_ by Taro Yashima or another story about Japan.

2.
Practice making Japanese characters that are in the book.

3
Find out about Japan. Where is it? How many people live there? What special customs do they have?

4
Make a Japanese scroll.

5
Practice the art of Japanese paper folding, origami.

JAPAN

by _____

Materials

Provide an umbrella contract for each child.

1 Provide the book *Umbrella* by Taro Yashima. This book is published by Puffin Books. For children who are slow readers, you may tape-record the story. Students may follow along as they listen. You may also choose from a host of other fine books about Japan.

2 Have available black felt tipped pens or small paint brushes and black paint for the children. Reproduce the Japanese ideograms vertically on white construction paper that has been cut into strips 6" x 18". The ideograms can also be used by children in writing stories.

3 Provide several reference books about Japan as well as maps, charts and any pictures you may have. These may be set up as part of a display about Japan along with objects from the country. Children may decide what aspect of Japanese life they would like to find out about. Children may write their finished facts as reports or do oral reports.

4 Provide two cut strips 2" x 6" black construction paper for each child. Each child glues the strips to the top and bottom of the white paper done in activity 2. Punch two holes in the top black strip 1" from each end. An 8" colored yarn strip may be tied to the two holes so that the finished scroll can be hung up in the classroom.

5 Provide several pieces of lightweight colored paper for each child. The pieces should be precut into various sizes of squares. Have available several library books on origami (Japanese paper folding) such as *Origami in the Classroom* by Araki which is published by Charles E. Tuttle Publishers. Children will enjoy folding origami figures as shown in the books. When a child has completed several figures, they may be converted into origami mobiles. Hang the figures with string or yarn from sticks, branches, clothes hangers or dowels.

AMERICAN INDIAN

1. Read the book <u>Arrow to the Sun</u> by Gerald McDermott or another story about Indians.

2. Make your own graph design.
   You need:

3. Make your own Pueblo village.
   You need: pipe cleaners Paper-Mache

4. Make a corn muffin!
   BISQUICK CORN-MEAL MILK

5. You need:
   Make your own sand painting.

by _____

1 Provide a contract for each child.

2 Provide copies of the book *Arrow to the Sun* by Gerald McDermott. This book is published by Puffin books. Those children who are slow readers can read along from a story you can provide on a tape cassette. The story has also been made into a film which is available through many of the centers from the county office of schools. In addition, there are many other fine books to choose from.

Provide graph paper (four or five to the inch) and thin felt tipped pens for each child. After examining the graph designs in the book, children may make their own designs. Designs that mirror each other are particularly effective and will make colorful additions to your classroom mounted with paper frames.

3 Each child (or a group of children) will need at least three small boxes of various sizes. The boxes will be stacked on top of each other and then taped into place. Small windows may be cut out of the boxes or later depicted by painted black squares. Cover the boxes with quick-drying papier mache (available in hobby and craft shops) and let them dry at least one day. On the following day the boxes may be painted with flesh-colored paint. Small ladders may be made out of pipe cleaners or by gluing small toothpicks together. Pueblo Indian people may also be made out of pipe cleaners or cardboard and added to the display. As each Pueblo house is completed, it may be placed in a designated area in the room for a Pueblo village.

4 Corn is such an important part of the Pueblo Indians' lives. If possible bring in pieces of Indian corn and display in the classroom. Each child may make his own cornmeal muffins by following the recipe that appears on the following page. You will need to supply the following materials: sugar, cornmeal, Bisquick, milk, eggs, muffin papers, an assortment of teaspoons, mixing bowls (small margarine tubs serve nicely) and stirring utensils (such as Popsicle sticks). Whip a tablespoon of water with the egg. Bake the finished muffins in a 350 degree oven for several minutes until done. Serve them plain or with butter and honey.

5 Provide a sheet of sandpaper for each child. Children may help provide the materials by bringing them from home. Children sketch designs onto the sandpaper lightly with pencil. The designs may then be colored by using bright-colored tempera paints or colored felt pens.

How to Make Cornmeal Muffins

SUGAR — ¼ teaspoon

1 teaspoon — CORNMEAL

BISQUICK — 1 tablespoon

MILK — 1½ teaspoons

egg — 2 teaspoons

Stir

Pour and Bake!

CHINA

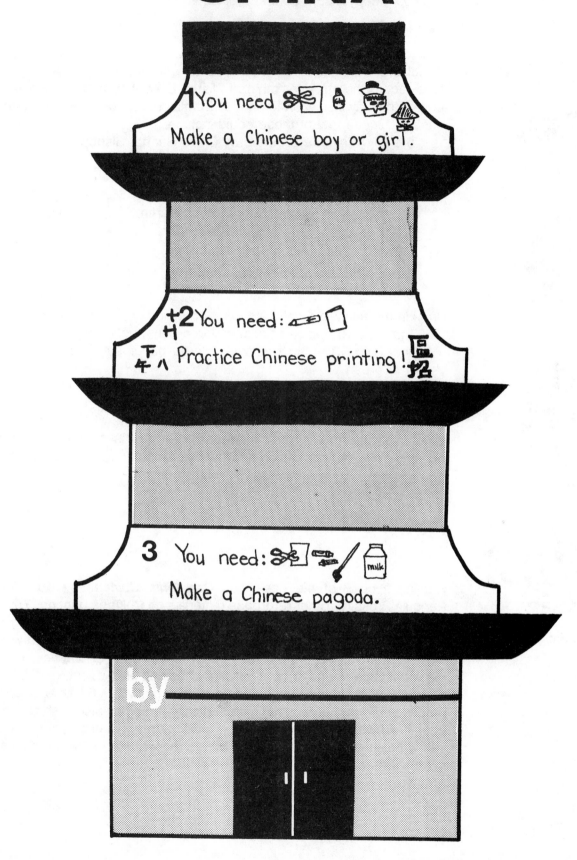

1 You need ✂️ 🍶 👦 👒

Make a Chinese boy or girl.

+2 You need: ✏️ 📄

Practice Chinese printing!

3 You need: ✂️📄 ✏️ 🖌️ 🥛

Make a Chinese pagoda.

by _____

Materials

Provide a copy of the contract for each child.

Provide copies of the book *Tikki, Tikki, Tembo* by Arlene Mosel, Scholastic Book Services. For children who are slow readers, you can tape-record the story for others to listen to as they follow along with the book. You may also wish to choose from a number of books as alternative choices. Just a few of these could include:

The Five Chinese Brothers by Claire Huchet Bishop
Meil by Thomas Handforth
The Pot Bank by Yen Liang
Moy Moy by Leo Lionni
The Rice Bowl Pet by Patricia Miles Martin

Provide the following materials for each child:

One 9" x 10" piece of flesh-colored construction paper

One 10" x 3" strip of bright-colored paper such as orange, pink, yellow or green.

One 3" x 3" piece of paper different from the color chosen above, one 2" x 2" piece of red paper, one 9" x 3" strip of black paper.

Two 2½" x 1" strips of paper the color of one of the colors above. Glue and scissors will also be needed. Provide a sample of the Chinese boy and girl as shown. Children follow the sample to complete the product.

Provide a copy of the book *You Can Write Chinese* by Kurt Wiese, Penguin Press, or other reference materials on Chinese printing. You may wish to invite a guest speaker or parent who can demonstrate Chinese ideograms to visit the class and display his ability. You may also wish to make a chart displaying the ideograms for children to practice. Provide black felt tipped pens or small paintbrushes and black paint for children to draw with. Cut strips of white construction paper 18" x 6" for each child to practice making the ideograms on vertically. You may also wish to provide each child with a booklet of stapled blank pages. On each page the child can write an ideogram and then illustrate the word in the space above using crayons or felt tipped pens.

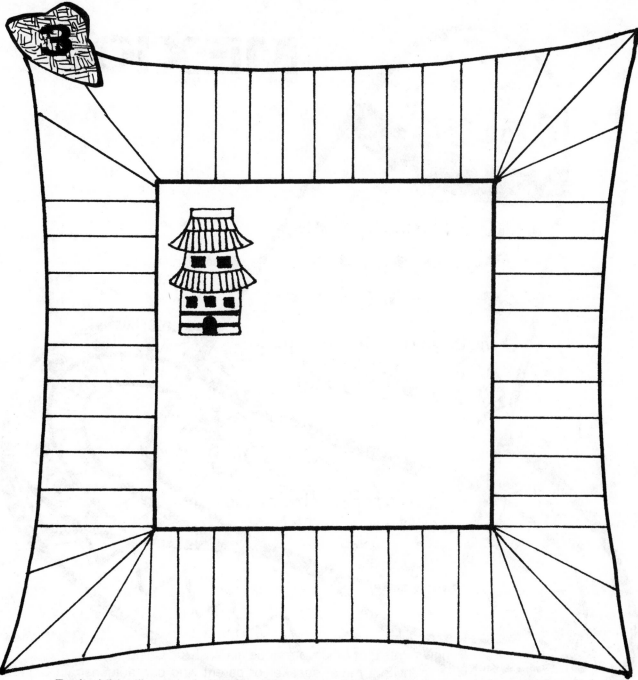

Each child will need a half-gallon milk carton. Cartons may be painted with bright colors by mixing a little detergent into the paint. The paint will then adhere to the waxy carton. Make a stencil of the balcony that appears on this page. Run off enough copies on bright-colored construction paper so that each child has at least two balconies. Children cut the balconies out and trace over the lines with black crayon or a felt tipped pen. The finished pagodas may be added to a classroom scene depicting *Tikki, Tikki, Tembo*. Additional figures may also be made. These can include:

    a well made out of clay and covered with small pebbles
    a ladder made out of pipe cleaners or toothpicks
    small tissue-paper flowers
    small paper junks
    Chinese children made from cardboard, pipe cleaners or spools.

MEXICO

1 Make a piñata!

2 Make a Mexican necklace!

3 Make your own serape!

4 Make a paper flower to wear at the fiesta!

by_____

Materials

Your class will enjoy having their own Christmas posada as they follow the tale of Ceci in the book *Nine Days to Christmas* by Marie Hall Ets, Viking Press. Many other fine books are also available about Mexico that you may choose from.

Provide varying sizes of paper bags depending on the number of children working on the project. Fill the bags half full of wrapped candy and shredded newspaper. Tie the top of the bags tightly with strings. Cut strips of colorful crepe paper in 5" widths. Children can fringe the paper by making cuts in 4" strips along the full lengths on the paper. Each strip is then fastened along the width of the bags by adding glue to the top edges of the strips. Add each additional fringed strip to the bag by overlapping it at least one inch. The finished pinata may then be strung up in the classroom to be used for the party. You may also enjoy reading *Pinatas* by Virginia Brock, Abingdon Press.

Each child can make her own necklace to wear with her serape. You can precolor the "beads" at home by using large hollow macaroni. Mix different food colorings with rubbing alcohol in separate jars. Color the beads and set them on wax paper to dry. Children can string their own necklaces on long strips of yarn.

Each child will need an old white sheet 46" x 26." A vertical slit will need to be cut in the center of each sheet for heads to fit through. Small ¼" slits may be cut one inch from the bottom of both sides of the serape by folding the material in and making small cuts. Pieces of colored yarn are drawn through each slit and tied together in knots along each small slash for fringe. Brightly colored designs may be added to the serapes by using bright-colored tempera paint.

Paper flowers will be colorful additions to wear or decorate the party with. Provide seven or more sheets of 7½" x 10" colored tissues and a 12" strip of yarn for each flower and follow these steps:
    Step 1: Lay all the sheets on top of each other.
    Step 2: Fold the sheets back and forth like a fan.
    Step 3: Tie a strip of yarn in a knot in the middle of the fan.
    Step 4: Pull each flower strip straight up and continue pulling the rest of the layers apart.

FIESTA TIME:

String up the pinata in a wide open space. Have a kerchief ready to use as a blindfold and a stick of some sort to hit the pinata with. Blindfold each child as he has a turn. Turn the child around three times and let him try to hit the pinata open to get the candy. Children can wear their serapes, necklaces and flowers at the fiesta. You may wish also to have children learn the Mexican Hat Dance and make some authentic Mexican dishes to sample.

RUSSIA

by _____

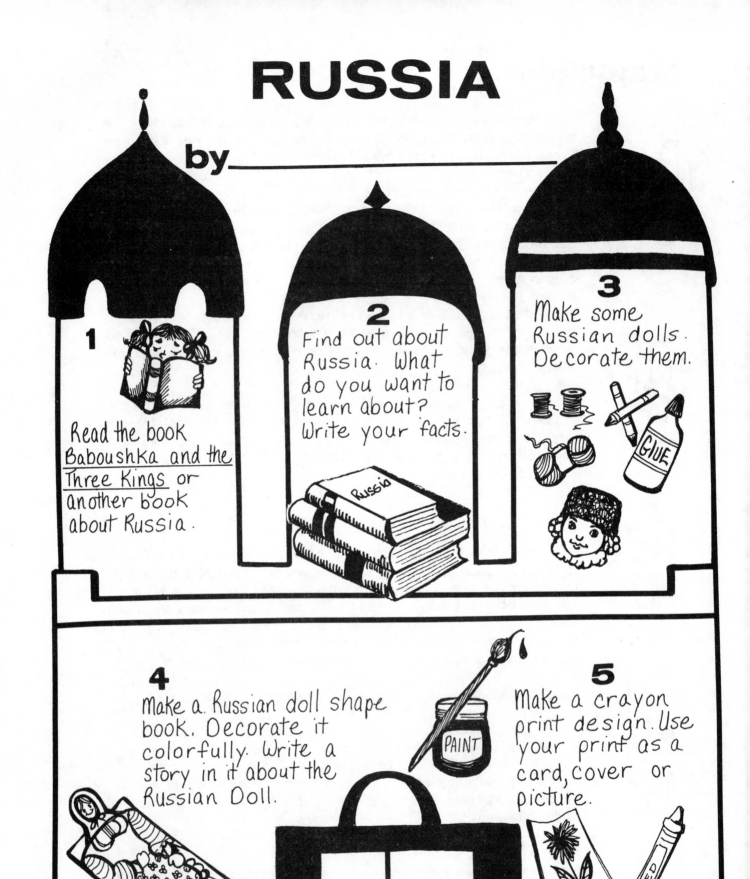

1 Read the book *Baboushka and the Three Kings* or another book about Russia.

2 Find out about Russia. What do you want to learn about? Write your facts.

3 Make some Russian dolls. Decorate them.

4 Make a Russian doll shape book. Decorate it colorfully. Write a story in it about the Russian Doll.

5 Make a crayon print design. Use your print as a card, cover or picture.

Materials

1   Provide an adequate number of contracts for students to use.

2   Provide copies of the book *Baboushka and the Three Kings* by Ruth Robbins, published by Parnassus Press. Children who are slow readers can listen to a tape you have recorded for the story as they read. You may choose many other fine stories about Russia such as *Stone Soup* or *The Big Turnip* or others as alternatives.

3   Provide an assortment of spools in varying sizes. Children can help provide the materials by bringing some from home. If possible, display Russian wooden stacking dolls and other Russian wooden figures. Children use at least three spools of varying sizes. Using thin-tipped felt pens, children color wooden dolls. You can also provide some of the following materials for children to decorate their dolls: cotton, sequins, feathers, wallpaper material, glitter and ricrac.

4   Duplicate an adequate number of pages of the Russian doll shape book for student booklets. To eliminate facial features from booklet pages, make a second stencil containing only the outline of the doll. Provide scratch paper for story drafts. Have scissors, pencils, crayons and a stapler available. Children can decorate their covers with crayons or felt tipped pens. Pages of writing paper for each book should be duplicated. Older students or volunteer parents can "cut-to-shape." Children can each write a fictional story about the Russian doll telling what adventures she experienced.

5   Cover a food warming tray with a sheet of aluminum foil. When the tray is warm, the child may make a crayon design on the foil using several different colors. Provide cut sheets of white construction paper at the center. To make the paint, the child lays the paper down over the crayon design. With oven glove potholders on, the child carefully smooths the paper down and then lifts it up for the finished product. The prints may be used as covers for the Russian reports. Framed with paper mats, they will make colorful displays in the room. They could also be pasted onto folded pieces of colored construction paper for cards. This is an activity that will need adult supervision!

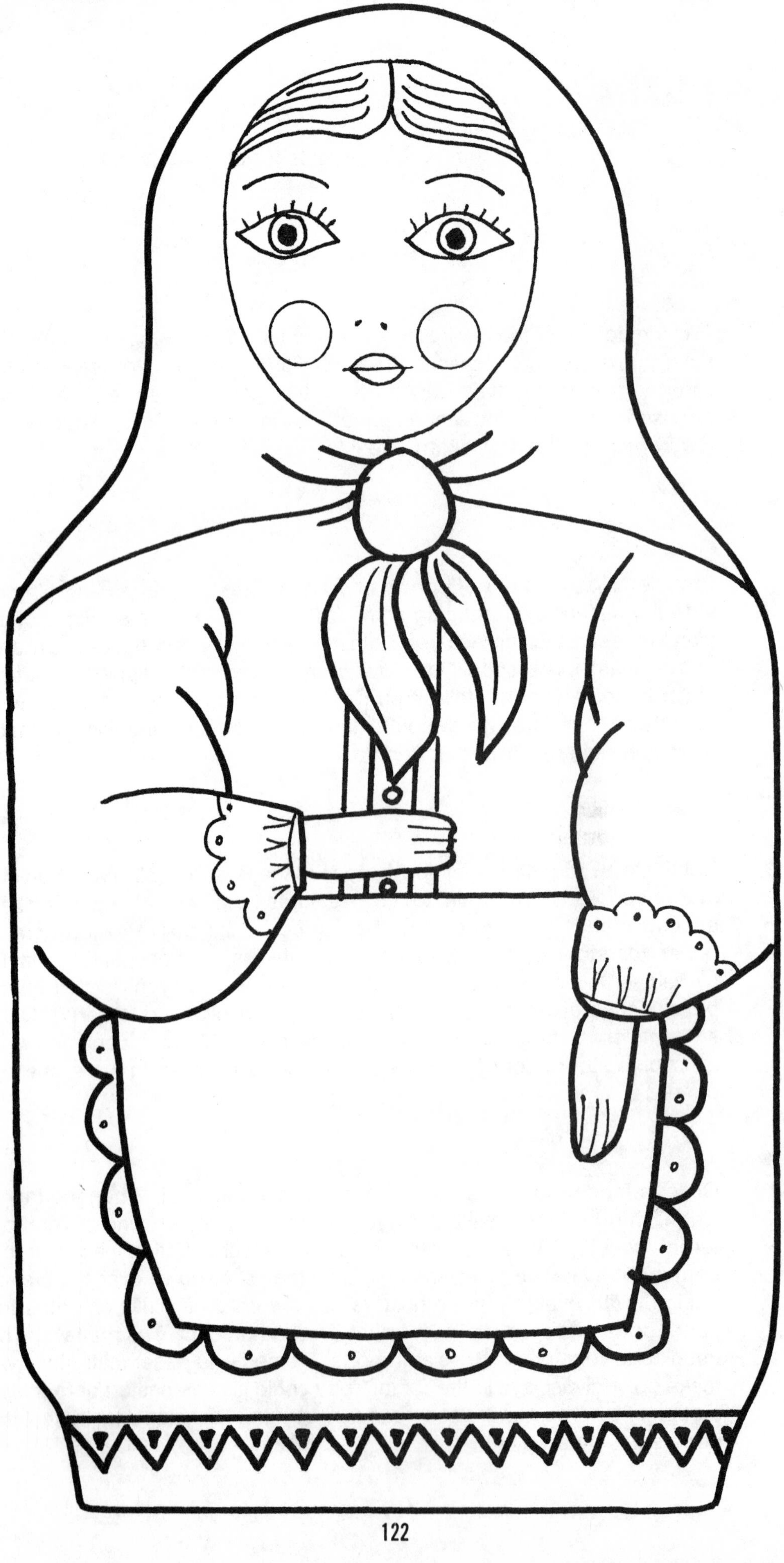